# AS A WITNESS TO THE LIGHT

# AS A WITNESS
# TO THE LIGHT

*The Story of Chengelo School
in Zambia 1988 – 2004*

Jeremy Collingwood

**Terra Nova Publications**

First published in Great Britain in 2006 by
**Terra Nova Publications International Ltd**
**PO Box 2400, Bradford on Avon, Wiltshire BA15 2YN**

Registered Office (not for trade):
21 St Thomas Street, Bristol BS1 6JS

Cover design by Roger Judd

Front cover photograph by Charles Alford
Other photographs by Keith Rushby and the author

ISBN  1 901949 41 9

Printed in Great Britain
by Bookmarque Ltd, Croydon

# Contents

# INTRODUCTION

Today Chengelo School is recognised as one of the leading schools in Africa. It has an enrolment of over 250 students in its secondary department, and some 100 children in its primary school. A sixth form offering A-levels in ten subjects was opened in January 2000. Its academic results would be the envy of many schools in the developed world. In 2003, 92% of pupils gained five or more passes at Grade C or above in Cambridge University's IGCSE examinations, and 40% of passes were at A* or A grades. On the sports field the boys' soccer 1st XI are regularly unbeaten, and Chengelo can usually hold its own in athletics, swimming, netball and basketball. Its Outdoor Centre at Ndubaluba provides opportunities for students to go camping, hiking, orienteering, canoeing, rock-climbing and abseiling. Many pupils do the bronze, silver or gold levels for the International Youth Award (the equivalent of the Duke of Edinburgh Award in Britain). Above all Chengelo is a Christian school where students are taught Christian values and encouraged to consider the Christian faith for themselves. On the Chilongoma Hills overlooking the school campus is a large wooden cross which symbolises the mission and purpose of Chengelo School.

Zambia is a big country as large as France, Switzerland, Austria and Hungary combined. It covers some 750,000 square kilometres and lies in the tropical belt of South Central Africa, 10 to 18 degrees south of the Equator. Its tropical heat is however tempered by its altitude, because most of the country occupies a high plateau of about 1,300 metres above sea level. On this high central plateau the predominant vegetation is savannah woodland.

The nation is shaped like a large butterfly. Until the railway connecting Zambia with Tanzania was built by the Chinese in the 1970s, the main line of rail and road lay up the central spine of the country stretching from Livingstone in the South to Ndola and Kitwe on the Copperbelt. Halfway up this main line of rail lies the capital Lusaka. Chengelo is situated in Mkushi District off the Great North Road, which runs up the right hand wing of the Zambian butterfly. Mkushi lies at a distance of some 200 kilometres from the Copperbelt and some 300 kilometres from Lusaka.

It was in 1964 that Zambia attained independence from Britain with a very small stock of educated manpower. At that time there were 100 Zambian graduates, a bare 1500 Zambians with a school Certificate, and only 6,000 who had had as much as two years of secondary education.[1] One party rule came to an end in 1991, when the President, Kenneth Kaunda, was peaceably voted out of office. The current President Levy Mwanawasa, who took over from Frederick Chiluba, on his election in 2002 launched an anti-corruption campaign.

Zambia is a peaceful but poor country, formerly highly dependent on copper, which at independence amounted to 90% of its exports and 50% of its government revenues. With the collapse in the copper market, Zambia entered a period of rapid economic decline, exacerbated by the closure of its southern border following UDI in Southern Rhodesia. Zambia has attempted to diversify and its exports today include copper (55%), cobalt, electricity, tobacco, maize, flowers and cotton. Higher copper prices and a doubling of the maize harvest in 2003 have helped to boost GDP by 4%. Tourism is showing significant improvement largely at the expense of Zimbabwe. But in 1993 86% of the population were said to live below the poverty line, and currently 50% are reckoned to be unemployed. External debt repayments have drained away large parts of the national wealth. But Zambia is now under the HIPC (Heavily Indebted Poor Countries) regime, and the national debt, which stood at over US$5bn, should be gradually written off in the next few years. 1.8 million people are estimated to be living with HIV/AIDS. This pandemic has brought life expectancy down to 42 years according to the Central Statistics Office, although the CIA Factbook gives a lower figure. With a birth rate of 3.6%, the population is predominantly youthful, and some 46.1% are children under 15 years of age.[2]

Zambia has a population of some 12 millions,[3] mostly concentrated in Lusaka and the Copperbelt. So why was the school built in the bush and miles from Lusaka and the Copperbelt? The answer to the question is that Chengelo is the brainchild of a small number of remarkable farmers who are members the Mkushi Christian Fellowship. It was to this Fellowship that the vision was first given to create a Christian secondary school at Mkushi. But what began as a Lilliputian scheme for a few correspondence-students has grown far beyond their wildest imaginations. David Moffat, one of the founding fathers, quips that what began as a vision and grew into a dream has ended in a nightmare. But he would be the first to acknowledge that what has developed out of the original vision has been a school of the highest excellence and a miracle of God's grace.

The story of Chengelo School is a story of faith. It is a story of faith challenged, stretched, and extended far beyond the comfort zone. At the outset the Lord gave the founders three promises: that they would never lack resources to build the school; that the school would be known throughout Zambia and beyond; and that in the years to come its pupils would have a significant impact upon Zambia. God has honoured the first two promises in a remarkable way, and there are good grounds for believing that over time Chengelo will have a truly significant impact upon the development of Zambia. The history of Chengelo School shows how God has proved to be faithful and trustworthy in all circumstances. And it is to God that the founding fathers would wish to ascribe all the praise and all the glory.

This account of Chengelo's history is not an official publication of Chengelo's Board of Governors or staff, nor of the Chengelo Educational Trust. It is written by a friend of Zambia and a supporter of the school, who has tried to give an honest and coherent account of Chengelo School over the past twenty years. It cannot claim to be a comprehensive record of all that has happened, and the author apologises for any mistakes or omissions. He is extremely grateful to all those who have assisted him in the writing of this history.

In particular the author wishes to thank the founding fathers and mothers of Chengelo, Russell and Anne Wyatt, David and Christine Moffat, and Barton and Yvonne Young, for their hospitality and assistance in ways too many to enumerate. He thanks Keith and Barbara Rushby for proof-reading and for lending their photographs of the school. He is very grateful to David Rust and Ruby Solomon, now Mrs Braumann, for making available contemporary letters.

Others who kindly agreed to be interviewed for the book include Roger and Angie Allen, Michael Chesterman, Peter Green, Mpundu and Leah Mutala and their son, David, John Ngulube, Melvyn Nolan, and Ian and Alison Richardson. Bob Baker, the late Jim Ford, John and Ruth Mellen, Mark Newhouse, Keith and Ida Waddell sent in useful contributions. Steve Baker gave me early encouragement to write the book and lent me a lot of useful material. Peter Snelson, an authority on the history of education within Zambia, kindly read through the text and gave me some helpful comments. My wife, Margaret, has made numerous suggestions, and has been a great encourager. Any errors are mine.

This book tells the story of Chengelo School up until the end of 2004. Andrew Cowling, the Headteacher of the secondary school, has kindly written a postscript for the year 2005.

*Jeremy Collingwood*
December 2005

PS Just before this book went off to the publisher, Russell Wyatt sent me the following quotation that he had read whilst laid up in bed. It speaks volumes for the spirit in which this whole enterprise was undertaken.

*'Following me (Jesus) is not like following some other masters. The wind sits always on my face and the foaming rage of the sea of this world, and the proud and lofty waves thereof do continually beat upon the sides of the bark (ship) that my cause, myself and my followers are in: he therefore that will not run hazards, and that is afraid to venture a drowning, let him not set foot into this vessel.'*

*John Bunyan*

**Notes**
[1] See Peter Snelson *Educational Development in Northern Rhodesia 1883–1945*, 2nd Edition, Kenneth Kaunda Foundation, Lusaka, 1990.
[2] For information on Zambia see www.cia.gov/cia/publications/factbook/geos/za.html
[3] Central Statistics Office. The CIA Factbook states population as 10.5 millions.

# Chapter One

# THE VISION

**Mkushi Christian Fellowship Retreat October 1985**
Where did it all begin? It seems that it was round the
Wyatt dining-table at the end of the retreat held by the
Mkushi Christian Fellowship (MCF) in October 1985. It
was there that Gordon Suckling first put the proposition
of a secondary school to Russell and Anne Wyatt and
David and Christine Moffat. 'I want your Fellowship to
consider whether God is calling you to start a Christian
secondary school in Zambia.' Gordon Suckling, a veteran
missionary in Zambia, was leading the retreat. He based
his Bible studies on the Book of Joshua —how Joshua
was commanded by God to lead his people across the
Jordan into the Promised Land. It was a venture pregnant
with danger and called for courage, leadership and faith.
Gordon challenged the members of the Fellowship as to
whether the people of God were willing to go forward
at God's calling into an unknown future trusting him for
provision, protection and guidance.

To start a secondary school in the heart of Africa is a
daunting task. It is difficult enough for a wealthy business
enterprise or even for a missionary organisation. But
it must have seemed well beyond the reach of a small

Christian fellowship, which at this time numbered only about 24 adults, mostly busy farmers. Then the task was made even more enormous when for one reason or another more than half the Fellowship began to disappear to other parts of the world. It must have felt a bit like Gideon felt when the Lord directed Gideon to reduce his army from 32,000 to 300 before battling the Midianites (Judges 7). But the Lord had not finished with this early testing of faith. The Fellowship had interpreted the challenge to start a secondary school in terms of a small residential group of pupils who would learn together following one of the recognised correspondence courses for O levels. So the original plan was only for a school of some 25 children in all, drawn mainly from the missionary and farming community. They could be accommodated in a hostel with houseparents, who would look after their pastoral and spiritual needs and oversee some basic sporting activities.

The Fellowship had a number of advisers. Geoff Wright was the first Headteacher of the King's School, Southampton. He and his wife, Norah, who was also a teacher, had worked in Zimbabwe training local African teachers. The Wrights had a clear view of what Christian education was all about and helped to implant their ideas into the thinking of the Fellowship. The Wrights met with members of the Mkushi Christian Fellowship on the 28th October 1986. Geoff Wright recommended a staff of three or four. They would be employed on a missionary basis, which would give them an adequate living wage and the costs of holidays within Zambia. He strongly advised against employing non-Christians on the staff. If only one couple was available, he suggested that to start with the school should use the Accelerated Christian Education programmed material for English Language, Maths and Science.

But God's vision was much bigger than the Mkushi Christians had yet contemplated. Heather Gibbs, the

Headmistress of Simba, a respected secondary school in Ndola, gave her opinion that in order for staff to offer an adequate coverage of subjects at 'O' level, two streams were necessary in a secondary school. But it was Peter Green who swung the whole argument and shook the Fellowship out of any cosy complacency about their proposed school.

## Peter Green's Intervention

Peter Green is a committed Christian and distinguished educationalist. As a young man he had overcome a limited formal education and severe tuberculosis to go on to study education and theology. He rose to become Vice-Principal of the College of St. Hild and St Bede in the University of Durham. Much of Peter's most important work has been done overseas. Beginning with trips to the Seychelles and Jamaica, Peter has worked in Lesotho and some 16 other countries in Africa and the Middle East. But it was Lesotho that came to dominate his overseas work for some twenty-one years. There he was involved in education, in preaching the word of the gospel and in development projects. It was the Basotho people who taught Peter that being one body in Christ involved sharing all that goes to make up individual lives. After many years the Basotho gave Peter one of their names, 'Ramosa', meaning 'Father of mercy and kindness.'

Peter was introduced to the Mkushi Christian Fellowship through his local church, St. Nicholas Durham, where Peter had worked with George Carey, later the Archbishop of Canterbury. It was a research student, Lawrence Moore, who mentioned to Peter that he had friends in Zambia, who wanted advice on starting a secondary school in Mkushi.

Lawrence Moore had taught at Treverton College in South Africa, where he was the class teacher for Mark Young, the son of a Mkushi farmer, Barton Young. Barton Young, together with Russell Wyatt and David Moffat, was to become one of the three founding fathers of the school. Following a prayer meeting with Russell and Anne Wyatt, and David and Christine Moffat, at the home of Barton and Yvonne Young, it was decided that Yvonne Young should write to Lawrence Moore in Britain to see whether he would consider the post of headmaster of the proposed school. Lawrence replied that he would accept provided that he did not get a bursary to study theology at Cambridge. As it happened, Lawrence did obtain a bursary for Cambridge and thus put himself out of the running for headmaster. But Lawrence Moore encouraged Christine Moffat, when on leave in Britain, to get in touch with Peter Green, as an expert on education in Africa. Thus it came about that Christine Moffat phoned Peter Green, who arranged to visit Zambia on his return from one of his regular trips to Lesotho.

Peter Green went and spent four or five days at Mkushi with Russell Wyatt, David Moffat and Barton Young. Russell Wyatt said that the school then consisted of a file about a quarter of an inch thick. Peter Green looked around and considered the prospects for a school. After some forty-eight hours he laid before the three farmers the basis of a school. He told them bluntly that their idea of a small residential school, whether based on correspondence or not, was simply not viable. In order to provide the range of subjects necessary for a proper secondary school, the Fellowship should be thinking in terms of some 250 students. This would be built up over five years with two classes of 25 each entering annually. The response was horror. David Moffat jests that Mkushi River (the first proposed name for the school) was a dream, and along came Peter Green and turned the dream into a nightmare. But as he readily admits the nightmare was to turn into a miracle of God's grace.

Peter Green presented his report to the Fellowship on the 1st December 1987. It was wide-ranging and detailed. Here is a summary of its main recommendations:

1. It is the task of the Board of Governors to develop the philosophy of the school, which would embody the Christian values of the Board. The school will then express those values in the content of its education. All Christian education is a process and is never complete.

2. The aim of the school should be simply stated, e.g. 'To provide a Christian education in Mkushi for children from 11 to 16 years'.

3. There is a minimum number of pupils at which the school could be financially and academically viable so that at GCSE the school would be able to offer a range of subjects to its pupils. Beginning in September 1988 with a roll projection of 57 pupils and three staff, Dr Green envisaged an expansion by September 1993 to 240 pupils and 10 to 12 staff[1] (allowing for a 10% drop-out at age 13).

4. The first three members of staff would be crucial to the development of the school because they would be the nucleus of all attitudes pervading the school. Dr Green recommended a mixture of local and overseas staff, building in a multi-ethnic element to the school.

5. Additional staff would include the Headmaster, who should have a light teaching load, an Administrator, and a Matron to be appointed in the second year.

6. The school was advised to employ a buildings officer, and a laboratory technician in 1991, as well as a librarian in due course. A specialist teacher in special learning education should be found for those with dyslexia problems.

7. Recommendations were made about the dining hall, a quiet place or chapel, the minimum cubic space per pupil, health and safety factors, and insurance cover.

8. Attention should be paid to the surroundings of the buildings to boost morale and promote the notion of excellence. The school needed to look cared for.

9. The International General Certificate of Secondary Education with its very new set of syllabi was

suggested. They had been introduced into England to counter rote learning and memory training and to foster concept formation and development. It was not just 'talk and chalk' but required an active response and skilled teaching.

10. The suggested curriculum for September 1990 was English Language, French, Religious Studies, Geography, History, Maths, Computer Studies, Agricultural Science, Food Science, and Combined Science. This would give any child a choice of six subjects out of ten. In September 1991 if there was a staff of nine, separate courses in Physics and Chemistry could be introduced. Biology could be brought in in 1992, so that the school could drop the combined Science option.

11. Dr Green offered advice on proposed Bye-laws for the Board of Governors.

12. It was suggested that universities in South Africa and Britain be invited to donate any equipment no longer in use.

To the eternal credit of those Christian farmers they turned their back on their little correspondence school and took up the new challenge that Peter Green had laid down for them. Russell Wyatt says of those days, 'Our vision had been quite small —far too small to be viable.' So they embarked on the new project. Russell again comments, 'We felt that we were crazy. Humanly speaking we were biting off far more than we could chew.' But the Fellowship was bolstered by what they took to be the Lord's confirmation that they should indeed proceed. Alan Scotland came out on a preaching tour and said, 'You're talking about it. Why don't you get on with it?' Then a Dane, Viggo Jensen, who was working for Barton Young said almost exactly the same thing.

Who are these three farming families to whom the vision and its implementation were committed? They are Russell and Anne Wyatt, Barton and Yvonne Young, and David and Christine Moffat. To understand the history of

Chengelo it is necessary to know something about each of these families.

## Russell and Anne Wyatt

The Wyatts arrived in Mkushi in July 1980, when they took over Sir John Moffat's farm, Kapanda. Russell Wyatt came out to Northern Rhodesia from West Sussex in 1947. His father was an astute farmer, who bequeathed a profound Christian influence to Russell. Russell was then a young man aged 19 years on an adventurous look-see. Initially he went to work with ffolliot Fisher on his farm in the Mwinilunga district of North-Western Zambia. Anne Fisher was one of the first people whom he met in this new land and at the end of 1950 they were married. Anne came from one of the longest-serving missionary families in the country.

Anne's grandfather, Dr Walter Fisher, a winner of the gold medal for surgery at Guy's Hospital in London, had come out to Africa as a missionary in 1889.[2] He was one of a party of thirteen Brethren missionaries recruited in Britain by the great missionary pioneer, Frederick Stanley Arnot. Arnot can be credited with setting up the very first school in Zambia. In March 1883 he recruited three small boys as pupils for his school in Limulunga at the court of the Litunga of Barotseland. Walter Fisher's sister, Harriet Jane, became the wife of Arnot. The small missionary band under Arnot was much ravaged by sickness and death. They cannot have been encouraged in confidence by memories of the fervent prayer of one of their supporters at a conference before their departure from England. Brother Nobbs had prayed in a deep sonorous voice, 'Lord, if they are too many for Thee to work with, thin them.' This zealous prayer was repeated three times. It proved to be prophetic. One missionary died on the voyage and two others died on the journey inland from Benguela. Arnot himself became so ill that Fisher advised him to return home. Accompanied by

Fisher and Anna Darling, Arnot and his wife retreated to Luanda, where Arnot recovered. Walter Fisher and Anna Darling were married before the British Consul in Luanda. After working for a time at Kwanjajula in Angola, Fisher and his wife moved further inland to join Cyril and Annie Bird at Kavungu in January 1914.

But Kavungu was unhealthy and the Birds' only child died after a few weeks and the Fishers' second girl after a few hours. In 1895 the Fishers had a son born, William Singleton, who was later to do much translation work. When the Fishers returned from furlough in August 1898, malaria was still causing much ill-health. They moved to Kazombo on the right-hand bank of the Zambezi in May 1899. Fisher was doing medical and building work and translating the Bible into Luvale. During his furlough Fisher had discussed malaria with experts in England. In consequence he now began to prescribe quinine as a prophylactic and not just as a treatment for malaria. This greatly reduced its incidence and almost entirely prevented blackwater fever. In 1906 the Fishers left Kazombo for Kalene Hill in Lunda-land, now Mwinilungu district. They worked there for nearly 30 years.

A hospital was built at Kalene Hill, which was to become one of the best known in the country. In 1914 an orphanage came into being, at one time the largest in the country. There was also the 'Witcherie' where unwanted, unloved old women were lovingly cared for. In 1928 Dr Fisher became incapacitated, losing power in his hands, and became more and more dependent on his wife. The 'good physician', the first missionary doctor in Zambia, died on 30th December 1935. He was buried in African fashion without a coffin. ffolliott Fisher went out to help his parents in 1920. He married Ethelwynne Marks from Mumbles, Swansea in 1921. He took up ranching and trading and contracting and settled at Hillwood Farm, about eleven miles from Kalene Hill. The orphanage work was moved to Hillwood Farm. ffolliott Fisher died in September 1966 and Mrs. Fisher carried on the work of the orphanage.

Gordon Suckling, the visionary thinker behind Chengelo, was the son of George Suckling who had gone out from London in 1911. Gordon Suckling married Peggy, a daughter of the ffolliot Fishers, and thus became a brother-in-law of Peggy's sister, Anne Wyatt. In 1955 Gordon and Peggy Suckling began a work at Loloma, an area on the Kabompo river east of Chitokoloki. Gordon then went into secular employment before returning to full-time missionary service. He and his wife settled in 1961 at a site by the Sachibondu river. There they had Bible schools, which were attended by African believers from a wide area.

Dr and Mrs Walter Fisher had left their family of six children to be educated in England, and one or other went home every two years to visit them. They prayed that a school might be provided for the children of missionaries in the 'Beloved Strip', that wide belt of territory, served by Brethren missionaries, stretching from Angola to Lake Tanganyika and straddling the borders of the Congo and Zambia. But it was not until 1922 that the Fishers received a gift earmarked for a school. Dr. Walter Fisher selected a beautiful site at Sakeji, some eleven miles south of Kalene Hill and a mile or more from ffolliott's farm. In 1972/73 there were 115–120 children at Sakeji. But since then numbers have greatly declined. Nevertheless the prayer of many Sakeji parents was that a secondary school on Christian lines similar to Sakeji might be established.

Russell Wyatt brought to the Chengelo project a background in agriculture and business. After spending time in Mwinilunga with the Fishers, he and Anne moved to Chingola and then Kitwe, where he developed one of the new state ranches, and was involved with Anne's uncle, Dr Charles Fisher, on his farm. On the Copperbelt Russell was much respected as a wise and statesmanlike elder in Christian circles. They moved to Lusaka where Russell became the livestock operations manager for

Zamanglo, a subsidiary of the Anglo-American company. Russell is a keen cattle breeder, particularly of registered Sussex cattle and later of Jerseys. In his time Russell has served as Chairman of the Herd Book Society of Zambia, Chairman of the Beef Cattle Producers and Director of Livestock Services Co-operative. When Russell and Anne moved to Mkushi they had no idea what God had in mind for them, apart from farming. They were generally looking forward to a quiet life and entering into a stage of semi-retirement. But that retreat in October 1985 was to change all their plans and thinking. From there on there was to be no going back. It was advance or failure.

**Barton and Yvonne Young**
The second member of the trio was Barton Young, who came to Mkushi from South Africa as a young man in 1957. He too can claim a mission heritage. One grandfather came out from Northamptonshire to work as a missionary in the Northern Cape not far from Kuruman. Barton's father and uncles found themselves out of sympathy with the apartheid regime established in South Africa after the Second World War, and Barton, after completing agricultural college, was encouraged to seek his fortune up north. Zimbabwe, or Southern Rhodesia as it then was, was too expensive for a young man aged 21 setting up in farming. So Barton and a friend headed north across the Zambezi. After visiting the Lands Board in Lusaka they arrived in Mkushi in a pick-up equipped with little more than some maps. They camped on the block and looked around and Barton found the land, which is now his farm. In order to set up in farming the Government required that a settler should have some £1,500 in equipment and £2,000 in cash. This was a lot of money but Barton used his undoubted charm to persuade a rugby friend to stand guarantee for him.

So Barton set about clearing and developing a virgin farm. In order to encourage commercial farming, the

Northern Rhodesia Government offered £1.10 for every pound invested by the settler. Barton's mother and father came to visit and as they stood either side of the tractor on which Barton was sitting, his father said that, although he could not give him any money, he would pray for God's blessing on his son and on his future life. This blessing on the son, a tradition going right back to the Hebrew Bible, was to greatly encourage Barton in the difficult times that lay ahead. His father told Barton, 'God's given you a gift to be creative, so use it.'

Barton says, 'When I look back on the hard days, I can see God's blessing. I started under a tree and lived in a stick house like an African, then I lived in the back of my tobacco sheds and moved on from there. I had bad years and nearly went bankrupt. For four years I lived under a debt adjustment scheme when I lost a lot of money on tobacco.'[3] Barton hated growing tobacco. He made a private commitment to the Lord in 1967: '"Lord if you can help me, I will never again grow tobacco." That year there was a shortage of potatoes down south. A friend of mine gave me support to buy potato seed and I grew a fantastic crop and I was able to pay my debt back.'

Barton is immensely proud of his three sons and six grandchildren. Another great love has been the breeding of pedigree cattle, including Brahman and Boran. His study is festooned with awards for his cattle and he has built an international reputation as a cattle judge, travelling to Namibia, Zimbabwe, South Africa and Kenya for this purpose. Recently he has started his own wildlife park with kudu, puku, impala, eland, waterbuck, sable antelope, oribi, hartebeest, and now giraffe. Barton feels too a great mission to preserve Zambia's indigenous trees. Many of these, such as misuku, mpundu, misamba and mutondo are to be found in his Noah's Ark Sanctuary, where he takes a great pride in showing local schoolchildren the flora and fauna.

But the biggest factor in Barton's life is undoubtedly his

love for Christ. As a young man Barton was the archetypal farmer, rugby-playing, hard-living and fun-loving. But his priorities underwent a fundamental shift when he met God. It was an itinerant Pentecostal preacher who opened the young Barton's eyes to the gospel. He underwent a genuine conversion and went down to the river and was baptised. Barton says, 'The Lord gave me salvation and for three months I could not leave my Bible alone. ...I prayed to the Lord that he would give me a brother to worship with. That same day, David Moffat came along. I was busy by the fire reading my Bible. And I said, "David, are you a Christian?" And he said, "Yes, why do you ask?" I said, "David, I have just been converted and I have been praying to the Lord to give me a Christian brother with whom I can pray and worship."'

So was born the Mkushi Christian Fellowship, or at least it was re-born since it had a prior existence under David's parents and uncles and aunts. Some time later Barton married Yvonne. Yvonne's great-grandmother, Mrs Landsberg, arrived in Bulawayo in November 1896 having delivered her daughter, Margaret, by the side of a wagon without doctor, nurse or anaesthetic. Yvonne's grandfather worked for Rhodesia Railways in the Southern Province and in Broken Hill (now Kabwe). Yvonne herself grew up in Kitwe and after her marriage she was baptised on confession of her faith in the Lord Jesus Christ at Kalwa, Serenje, in 1975. David Moffat in the meantime had got married to Christine Sewell and in David's words 'the congregation doubled'.

**David and Christine Moffat**
David Moffat is a direct descendant of the pioneer missionary, Robert Moffat of Kuruman, who had gone out to South Africa in 1816 with the London Missionary Society. Robert's eldest daughter, Mary, married David Livingstone in 1845. David is descended from Robert's eighth child, John Smith Moffat, who worked first as a

missionary before entering government service. John Smith Moffat's son, Malcolm, became a missionary with the Church of Scotland, and opened a mission station at Chitambo in 1907.[4] He was later joined by Dr Hubert Wilson, a grandson of Livingstone. Chitambo, on the edge of the Benguela Swamps in Zambia, is where David Livingstone had died in 1873, and where his faithful servants buried his heart before carrying his body back to the coast. Chitambo, a mosquito-riven area, proved to be an unhealthy site for a mission station and Malcolm Moffat moved the station to a healthier spot on the plateau some 80 kms from the present Serenje and some 186 kms from Mkushi in 1910.

Malcolm Moffat had three sons, Unwin, John and Robert. All were to play a distinguished part in the government and development of what was then Northern Rhodesia, a protectorate under the British Crown. Sir John Moffat, as he became, was a district commissioner and one-time Secretary for Native Affairs, who went into politics and became one of the founder members of the Liberal Party. He was the author of the so-called Moffat Resolutions designed to safeguard racial parity and equality within the territory. With the rise of African nationalism, and in particular of the United Independence Party under Kenneth Kaunda, the Liberal Party found itself swept aside. In 1971 Sir John Moffat and his wife Peggy retired to Scotland, and after one year relocated to New Zealand. Robert Moffat became the legal adviser to the Colonial Government on African customary law. Robert and his wife, Margaret, retired to Scotland.

David's father, Unwin Moffat, was an agriculturalist. In the late 1940s he conducted a government survey of land in the Mkushi district. At that time the area, which was to become the Mkushi farm block, was a region of largely uninhabited and uncontrolled bush. The block was Crown land and the Moffat survey divided it into farms of between 2,000 and 6,000 acres. But few settlers were attracted mainly because the farms were 70 to 80 miles away from the line of rail and the roads were bad. But the Moffat brothers saw the potential of the area and moved in to clear the land. In 1956 the Federal Government subdivided the land into smaller, intensive tobacco farms of some 1,000 to 2,000 acres each. In May 1965, there were some 80 commercial farmers on the block.[5]

When interviewed in Horizon magazine in May 1965, Unwin Moffat said, 'It is strange seeing all these folk. When we did the survey there was no one here. We found the occasional hunting camp but that was all. No one had tried to grow tobacco and our plan was based on cattle. We put a stream on every farm and used watersheds as boundaries. Robert and John and I have cleared about 900 acres by planting 80 to 100 acres of tobacco a year and using the crop to pay the costs of clearance. But we have concentrated on cattle and at present have just under 1,000 head. ...Things have changed a lot. In the old days we would drive our cattle on the hoof down to the railway at Kapiri Mposhi, or even as far as Broken Hill (now Kabwe). ...There used to be a lot of game in the block. We have had an elephant walk within 100 yards of the house. When we first settled here lions and leopards often came after the stock. One year lions killed eleven of our animals. My brother John shot the last lion on New Year's Day two years ago. ...In 1962 we lost thirteen calves to one leopard. I remember that leopard very well. I was chasing up a hill trying to get a shot when I had a coronary thrombosis. We finally killed the leopard with poison.'

It was to this remote area of rural Africa that Unwin and his wife Sheila brought their family of four children, Malcolm (now a retired paediatrician in Scotland), Mary (married to a Church of Scotland minister), Flora (married to a business executive in England), and David. Flora can remember coming to the area in 1951 with the family. They lived under canvas next to the Chimya stream for some six months before moving to a wattle and daub house which was connected to one occupied by her uncle and aunt, John and Peggy. In those days there were lions and leopards and buck around. Once there was a massive lion-hunt after a lion killed several of the cattle. 'We all went and sat up a tree in the drizzle. Underneath was the carcase of one of the cattle. We giggled and were taken to account. We then heard the lion. One of the local farmers took an early and tentative shot, which wounded the lion, much to Uncle John's fury. The lion took off and Uncle John and father spent the next day tracking the lion.'[6]

After the wattle and daub hut, a brick farmhouse was built. David and Christine Moffat still live in that same farmhouse, Chimyamauni, which has changed little since Unwin's time. The house, which has only just gone on to mains electricity, is still fed with brownish water from the channel dug out by Unwin from the Mkushi river. This was where David grew up, and from where he took the train for the long journey of four or five days down to school in South Africa. David studied agriculture at the West of Scotland College of Agriculture in Glasgow. He returned to the farm to run the cattle for his father and his two uncles, before going overseas again to study agricultural engineering at Writtle College of Agriculture in Essex. He then taught for a while at the newly-formed Natural Resources Development College in Lusaka, before returning home to take over the family farm from his father. He married Christine (née Sewell), who had gone out to Zambia as a VSO to do nutrition work, and they have two children, Andrew, who is now working a neighbouring farm to his father's, and Catherine, a surgeon studying in England,

## God's Promises

Through all the testing days that lay ahead the three founding families were heartened by three clear promises from God, which were reinforced in letters and conversations with other Christians. These promises were to underlay the whole project. David Moffat summarised the promises as:

1. We would never lack resources to build the school.
2. We would be known throughout the country and beyond.
3. That in years to come pupils would have a significant impact upon Zambia.

But how would the reality match the vision?

**Notes**

[1] Dr Alan Staples of Treverton College did not agree with the proposed teacher:pupil ratio of 1:20. He noted that independent schools in South Africa have at best a ratio of 1:11 and at worst 1:15, including the headmaster and librarian with the teachers. These ratios give class sizes in the region of 20-25 pupils (letter to Russell Wyatt dated 31 October 1993). Ian Richardson was also advocating 16 teachers to give adequate options.

[2] For the Fishers, see Peter Snelson: *Educational Development in Northern Rhodesia, 1883-1945*, 2nd Edition, 1985, published by the Kenneth Kaunda Foundation, Lusaka, and *Turning the World Upside Down*, 2nd Edition 1973, published by Echoes of Service, Bath, Somerset.

[3] Interview with author 19.05.04.

[4] For Malcolm Moffat see Peter Snelson (1985).

[5] It should be noted that today in Zambia, all land is state land, some of which is let out on 99 year leases, for which farmers have to pay an annual land rent.

[6] Interview with author 16.05.04.

# Chapter Two

# The Reality

It is one thing to have a vision and a blueprint. It is another thing to turn that into reality. How do a few farmers create a first-class secondary school in the middle of the African bush? We can dream of a school, but when we wake up it is only a dream, and the truth is that on the ground all the teachers and pupils and desks and text books and sports fields have vanished, like a mist burnt up by the African sun. Peter Green's visit only prompted more questions. Where was the school to be situated? How to find the teachers? Where will the pupils come from? How much is this all going to cost? Who is going to find the money? How will the school be governed and on what principles? Will the Government approve the school?

**First Plans July 1986**
The Mkushi Christian Fellowship first went public with their plans for a secondary school the following year. A circular letter dated 16th July 1986 went out to potential supporters. It read:

*In response to a challenge which God has placed before us, we are initiating the establishment of a Christian secondary school here in Mkushi Farm Block. Not only do we see a great need for a school of this type in Zambia, but we feel this a very suitable area for such a project. Our vision is for a rapidly-growing school based on the highest Christian standards. The aim is to enable farmers, missionaries and Christian workers, expatriate contract workers and others who value this type of education to send their children to school within Zambia. We are looking for those who will stand with us in effective prayer and support.*

*The school is being designed as a boarding establishment, initially situated on David Moffat's farm at Lilanda house. Tuition at the start will probably be based on correspondence courses under the guidance of qualified staff. We hope to start in January 1987.*

*The premises are now being modified to accommodate staff and eight to ten children under the supervision of Terry Fisher. We have purchased five asbestos prefabricated classrooms of which two will shortly be erected. To date we have invested K45,000 in cash and a similar amount in kind. We are also in contact with people in England who are experienced in Christian education with a view to obtaining staff with a vision similar to ours.*

The letter indicates that the founding fathers were still thinking of a fairly modest school with limited boarding accommodation and with the syllabus based around correspondence courses. The site was to be on Nkolonga Farm, belonging to David Moffat. Lilanda had been the farmhouse belonging to David's uncle, Robert. In March 1986 Terry Fisher and his wife, Barbara, visited Mkushi on sabbatical leave from a Christian fellowship in the south of England. Terry prepared plans and drawings for the adapting of the Lilanda buildings for use as accommodation. Terry and Barbara were able to return in July and August to oversee the completion of stage 1 of the alterations.

It was Jim Ford, a long-standing missionary in Kabwe, who came up with the prefabricated classrooms. Jim and his wife Dorothy had heard of the proposals for a secondary school when on a preaching visit to Mkushi. Jim gives this account:

*A few weeks later Dorothy noticed in the Times of Zambia that some excellent prefabricated buildings were up for tender at the Broken Hill mine. She encouraged me to go and view these and I was astonished at the excellent quality of these buildings, which were large and well-equipped with built-in cupboards, and even one with laboratory fittings. I priced them as carefully as I could to a total of K100,000, which was at that time £50,000, and I telephoned David Moffat, and asked him if the farmers could raise that large sum as the next day was the deadline for the submission of tenders. He told me later that he went around the farms with his cap in his hand and was given the go-ahead by his colleagues. I put in the tender of K50,000 which I considered about half the value, and it was accepted with the condition that they could withdraw the largest buildings with the laboratory fittings. I phoned David again and he said, 'No, it is all or nothing.' Agreement was reached and now it was my task to clear all the buildings from the site within two weeks. I asked David Moffat if they could supply a daily truck to come from Mkushi, 130 miles distant, as this would enable my team and myself to get the buildings dismantled and transported.*

*So we began, and as my lads were taking down the buildings I was marking each sheet of iron or asbestos with the number of the building and the code number we gave for the re-assembly at Mkushi. It was a mammoth task, but we had everything down and away to Mkushi within the allotted two weeks, and miracle of miracles not a single sheet of asbestos was broken and all the cupboards were undamaged. It was at this point that David Souter came into the picture. With his building skills the farmers invited him to re-assemble the buildings and to lay down the slabs of concrete required, including the foundation of the school administration block. He took my workmen with him and they stayed at Mkushi for several weeks to do the job.*[1]

A somewhat different account appears in Chengelo: The First Three Years: 'Moffats and Wyatts carpenters were despatched to Kabwe with the strict instructions "take them apart carefully because you'll be the ones putting them together again." Duly dismantled and five lorry trips later, re-assembled, 3 classroom and 1 lab, finally stood. There were only two asbestos sheets and a couple of windows broken —quite incredible for 40-year-old buildings.'[2] Russell Wyatt favours this version and pays tribute to the skill and memories of the two carpenters who assembled the buildings bit by bit without mistake. So Chengelo got its classrooms. The first 50 desks were donated by Mr Eddie Mahtani from Ndola. Local carpenters were then hired to make the next batch of 100 desks.

In a second circular, dated 27th November 1986, the Fellowship reported that during the stay of Terry and Barbara Fisher, the modification and extension of the farmhouse, originally belonging to Robert Moffat, had been achieved to give boarding accommodation for eight girls and eight boys, a married couple and a single staff member. In addition two of the prefabricated classrooms had been erected. The classrooms would serve up to 48 children, that is day pupils as well as boarders. However to finish Stage 1, the plumbing and drainage for the staff suite had to be completed and the whole house painted. Two further prefabs would have to be erected. The Fellowship had reluctantly to accept that the school was unlikely to open in January 1987.

### The Search for a Head
In May 1987 the Fellowship reported that their hopes of finding a head of the school had been disappointed. As already mentioned, Lawrence and Irene Moore, who had taught at Treverton, a Christian school in South Africa, had expressed interest in Mkushi, but eventually decided to take up an opportunity to study theology in Cambridge. In

the meantime the Fellowship, having trawled in vain for some time for a suitable candidate, asked Geoff and Norah Wright, who had experience of Christian schools in Zimbabwe and Southampton, whether they would consider launching the school pending the appointment of a permanent head.

Work had now started on the second stage of the building modification plan. Farm building teams had enlarged the dormitory block behind the main house and there was an urgent need to make and burn additional bricks. Richard Bennett and his wife, Carol, from Norwich in England, were planning to visit to carry out the electrical installations throughout the complex. A solar panel had already been installed to provide power for some night-lights and a radio telephone. An answer to specific prayer for finance came when a cheque arrived for K6,000 two days after the Fellowship prayer time. There was still the hope that the school could open in September. A circular letter closed, 'Please pray for us here in Mkushi that the vision remains clear, that our faith does not waver, and that we may have patience as we wait for things to fall into place.' The Fellowship certainly needed faith and patience for it was to be over a year before the school could open.

Several months later the Fellowship could report that donations totalled K83,192, and that they had spent K59,333. However contributions in kind in the shape of labour, transport, bricks, cement, desks, a solar panel and the original buildings far exceeded this amount. There was an immediate need for hard and soft furnishings, kitchenware, cutlery and crockery, a stove, deep freezer, refrigerator, lighting plant, vehicle, educational and sports equipment, books and so on. Even butchery knives had to be purchased and Philip and Betty Sercombe found themselves having to scour the south of England for suitable equipment. The list of things to do and to acquire seemed inexhaustible. But the need for the school was more urgent than ever. In May 1987, the Zambian Government, faced with a deteriorating balance of payments situation, had imposed a ban on the externalisation of school fees for new pupils studying out of Zambia at both primary and secondary level.

## The Board of Governors

As time went on it became increasingly important to put the management of the school on a proper basis. No longer could this be done in private conversations or by calculations on the backs of envelopes. In October 1987 a meeting was held at the school buildings to discuss the formation of a board of governors. Those present included the three founding fathers, David Moffat, Russell Wyatt and Barton Young, Christine Moffat (who acted as Secretary), Traugott Hartmann and Brian Bentley. Brian Bentley, a Christian farmer from Mwinilunga, had at various times been Headmaster of Mwinilunga Secondary School and managing director of Fairway Engineering on the Copperbelt. Brian was later to join the staff of Chengelo and play a large part in its development. Traugott Hartmann was a long-standing missionary whose extensive contacts with German churches were to prove a boon for the nascent school. He is still a Governor today and is a Director of Life Trust, which runs an AIDS orphan/school project for more than 3,000 children in eight schools in and around Kabwe.

The minutes noted that a trust company, the Mkushi Christian Fellowship Trust Ltd was being set up with David Moffat, Russell Wyatt and Barton Young as trustees.[3] Once the trust had been formally registered it would have the advantage of charity status. The Board of Governors to be established would take responsibility for the appointment of the first Headmaster and other staff. It was agreed that the Headmaster would be an ex-officio, non-voting member of the Board. It was recommended that, in addition to those present at the meeting, Mpundu Mutala, the General Secretary of the Bible Society of Zambia, and Roma Nyakambumba of Christian Fellowships of Zambia should be invited to join the board.

The minutes also recorded that it was thought that somewhere between K10,000 and K15,000 was in hand. It was formally agreed as a matter of principle that the financial policy should be that the school would be built and equipped by donations, but that its running costs should come out of fees, covering costs with a small margin. The first fees would be set after a careful consideration of the estimated cost of running the school for one term. Bursaries should be funded from donations. It was questioned in the light of the progress made whether it was now urgent for Dr Peter Green to visit Mkushi on his return to Britain from Lesotho. Perhaps the most significant decision at the meeting was to invite one Neil Solomon and his wife to visit the school during the Christmas holidays probably at the beginning of January 1988.

The first formal meeting of the Board of Governors of Mkushi Christian Fellowship School was held on the 14th November 1987. The six members of the previous meeting, together with Mpundu Mutala and Roma Nyakambumba, were all present. Russell Wyatt was proposed and accepted as Chairman of the Board with Christine Moffat as Secretary.

## A Christian School
The Board accepted that the purpose of the school was to establish a first-class secondary school on a Christian basis for the children of Christian expatriates and nationals. It was hoped that the school would be a means of outreach for Christ into the community at large, one which would be a landmark for Christ and Christian principles, and from which would come leaders in all sections of Zambian life, particularly the Church. The concept of Christian education agreed by the Board was one where:

1. The knowledge of the Triune God of the Bible is regarded as essential to each child's proper physical, mental and social development.

2. God is acknowledged and taught as being the Creator and Controller of all things.

3. Each individual child is seen as having a specific value, as in the eyes of God, and therefore all types of gifts, abilities and personalities are given equal esteem, as well as opportunity and encouragement to develop.

4. God's moral standards are taught as unchanging and essential to the full realisation of a person's identity and security in life.

5. A broad range of educational opportunities are given in order to foster the differing qualities of each child.

6. The full-time staff are born-again believers in Jesus Christ and are committed to the above ideals.

At the Board meeting David Moffat most generously agreed that he would explore the legal issues of excising up to 200 hectares from his farm, with access from the district road, for the development of the school. It is interesting to note however, that even at this stage it was still believed that the residential complex attached to the redundant Mkushi Copper Mine might yet be the Lord's provision for the full development of the school. The founding fathers had been attracted to this campus from the first, but the receivers of the mine held out for what was to be an unrealistic price. The Seventh Day Adventists made an offer to buy the property but this sale fell through. In retrospect the site would have been very difficult for the founders to manage since it was sited some 90kms or more from their farms. Over time the mine complex went back to the bush.[4]

**A Witness to the Light**
In God's providence it became clear that a greenfield site based around the Lilanda farmhouse was the God-appointed site for the new school. But what was the

school to be called? The Governors favoured something equivalent to Beacon School, as the vision was that the school should be a beacon for Africa. It was Mpundu Mutala who came up with the Bemba name of 'Chengelo', which means 'Light'. Hence Chengelo School, as a witness to the light of Christ, was conceived. Conceived but not yet born.

In December 1987, Dr Peter Green, came to Mkushi, and after three days let drop the bombshell: the small-scale school planned by the founding fathers was just not viable, in terms of educational quality or financial sustainability. Instead he proposed a two-stream entry of 50 pupils each year from September 1988 building up to some 240–250 pupils by September 1993. Out of the window went any idea of correspondence education. Instead Peter Green recommended that the school should operate with direct classroom tuition. He also indicated that the school should work towards the Cambridge International General Certificate of Secondary Education (IGCSE). What was now required of the Governors and their friends was a total change in mindset, or a paradigm shift as theologians like to put it, from a cosy parochial school to a national institution. It would be hard to overstate the faith involved in the fact that the Board accepted Peter Green's report as definitive for the working-out of their vision.

## The Appointment of the Headmaster
But the engine for the new machine was not yet in place. A Headmaster had still not been appointed. It was Barton Young who, precisely at the right time, produced job applications and CVs from Neil and Ruby Solomon. Barton and Yvonne Young had a connection with Treverton College at Mooi River in the beautiful heartland of the Kwazulu-Natal Midlands in South Africa. Treverton aims to provide an all-round quality education based on a strong Christian foundation. Not only had Mark Young been

educated at Treverton, but the Youngs had a farm in the vicinity of Treverton, which they had lent to the College for various outdoor activities. As we have seen, Yvonne and Barton had written to Lawrence and Irene Moore, formerly on the Treverton staff, explaining Chengelo's need for a headmaster. Lawrence did not feel able to take up the offer when he obtained a place at Cambridge, but he did undertake to look around for a possible candidate.

Neil and Ruby Solomon from Treverton took a vacation in Scotland where they met up with the Moores in Edinburgh, and learnt about the proposed school in Mkushi. When Barton and his son Mark were next in South Africa, Neil, who had been Mark's English teacher, asked if he might meet with Barton. Over a cup of tea, Neil told Barton that the Lord had laid it on his heart to start a Christian school in Africa. Barton responded that he did not want to be seen pinching staff from Treverton. Neil then produced a letter addressed to the Treverton Headmaster, Dr Staples. Neil was resigning from the school because he wanted a challenge like that proposed in Mkushi. Barton Young told Neil candidly that things were not exactly easy in Zambia. The country in the latter years of the Kaunda presidency was in deep economic trouble, and there were massive shortages of basics such as sugar and flour. Ruby Solomon had come in during this conversation, and she put her hand on her husband's shoulder and said, 'Neil, if you are willing to take on this venture, I am ready to support you.' Barton then arranged to meet up with Neil Solomon on the mountain on his farm. So Barton and Neil went up together on the mountain and prayed about Chengelo.

Barton Young returned elated to Mkushi. The Mkushi Christian Fellowship was holding a retreat at Lilanda farmhouse. Barton first showed Neil's CV to Peter Pedersen, the Danish Principal of Kaniki Bible College, and then handed it to David Moffat and Russell Wyatt. Peter was known as a man of deep prayer who would fast and pray for many days if necessary. The next day when the founding fathers and others sat around the table having tea, Peter Pedersen said that he had read Neil's CV and he thought that he was the man for the post. There was enthusiastic support from those present. This meeting around the table on the 24th October 1987 went on to constitute the first meeting of the Board of Governors. So Neil and Ruby were flown up to Zambia. Barton met them in Lusaka and brought them up to Mkushi for the interview.

The Governors all felt in their spirits that Neil was the right man and that his coming was God-given. With Neil Solomon's application was a letter from the Principal at Treverton, Dr Alan Staples. Dr Staples wrote that Neil was invaluable but if God were calling him to Chengelo, then he would release him with God's blessing. For the Solomons themselves it was a brave move leaving the relative security of Treverton College to start a school from scratch in Zambia. Furthermore the concept of the school had also dramatically changed since Neil had first heard of it. It was not just to be a small correspondence-based school, but a full-scale secondary boarding school. But Neil had the advantage of bringing to Chengelo his experience of Treverton College with its well-established Christian ethos.

**The First Staff Arrive**

'The most important thing that you will do is to appoint your first three staff members. They will set the pace.' This advice from Geoff Wright from Southampton was to prove prophetic. Little by little the business of putting together the Chengelo jigsaw went ahead. The vital first three appointments of staff were the Solomons, the Rushbys and the Rusts.

The first to arrive were Keith and Barbara Rushby. They were designated as administrators and helpers. Keith was a retired Royal Navy officer. It was while they were helping at the Montgomery Care Centre in Zimbabwe that they first heard of Chengelo through Geoff and Norah Wright. The Wrights after they returned from Zimbabwe suggested to the Rushbys that they should consider offering for Chengelo. The Rushbys arrived from their home in Southampton in April 1988 and settled into their cottage. They became deeply involved in purchasing, stock control, labour supervision and correspondence. Barbara Rushby kept the school accounts 'down to the last ngwee'. However the Rushbys did not have work permits and had to return to the UK for a while until they were issued with the necessary authorisations.

Neil Solomon, the first Headmaster, and his wife Ruby, a science teacher-cum-mother-cum-general helper arrived at the school in June together with their two sons, Timothy and Luke.

David and Rachel Rust travelled from Britain on the 21st July with their three children, Rebecca, Jonathan and Helen. David was to teach History and French, and Rachel taught Mathematics. They became the first houseparents in the girls' hostel. The Rusts were not new to Africa having previously worked in Kenya before they were married. They had heard of Chengelo through Dave Day, one of the leaders of the Bristol Christian Fellowship, who often visited Zambia. The Rusts had taught at a Christian school in Bristol.

### The Builders

The new school campus became a scene of feverish activity. At this stage builders outnumbered the teaching staff. The farm building teams were supplemented by outside assistance. David and Marjorie Souter, missionaries from Dundee, who were working in Kabwe gave invaluable assistance in providing a building team for several months and in supervising the building work. Three men with experience in building and construction work came out from the Bristol Christian

Fellowship and gave help and guidance. Gordon Blower from Mobile Mission Maintenance (MMM), an Australian-based missionary service organisation, brought a team of seven men from the building trades to do roofing, plumbing, electrical, carpentry and internal fitting work. A Swedish lady, Annalee Ericksen, drew up the design of the hostel, which with subsequent modifications became the template for future use.

Christine Moffat counts the help offered by the Souters, MMM and Annalee Ericksen as divine provision. 'There was a time in March 1988 when we had just six months for opening and we had nothing. We had no materials and no builders. We had to have a hostel besides the farmhouse. ...Building materials were very hard to come by at that time. A local farmer who looked at our plans said that he had had an order in for roofing materials for 18 months. "You're not going to build that hostel in six months." But we did. That was very exciting when we saw such answers to prayer.'[5]

Work proceeded on adapting the farm manager's house for the Solomons, and in building a purpose-built hostel, of some 650 sq.m. for the boys, which was subsequently allocated for the girls. A water borehole, with excellent-quality drinking water, was drilled by a local farmer as his gift to the school. A water tower had to be built by September, as did domestic staff housing and a laundry. The Beit Trust[6] provided money for two electrical generators. The wives of the founding farmers were intimately involved with all the preparations for the school. Christine Moffat kept a record of income and expenditure as well as doing the correspondence and minutes for the Governors and staff. Yvonne Young brought her particular creative and home-making skills in choosing furniture and furnishings for the hostels and staff accommodation, and in organising the domestic staff. Anne Wyatt was having to take up the heavy responsibility of overseeing the catering and kitchen and laundry work. A full-time caterer was not to arrive until May 1989.

Chengelo was fortunate with its timing. The Kaunda Government had had a policy of putting all schools under government control. But with a worsening economic outlook it became increasingly apparent that the Zambian Government could not fund all the schools. The liberalisation of private education would remove some of the financial burden from the back of the public exchequer. Gradual encouragement was therefore given to the private sector of education, a process which was accelerated with the coming of the new Government under President Frederick Chiluba in 1991. At the same time as the Government was showing itself more favourable to private education, there was a growing demand for high-quality secondary education from both Zambians and expatriates. Many missionaries and key Christian workers were leaving the country or considering doing so, because of their dissatisfaction with the education available for their children within Zambia. So there was no lack of enquiries from parents. The Government showed itself to be sympathetic to the creation of a private school at Chengelo. On 8th December 1988, the Ministry of General Education, Youth and Sport confirmed that Chengelo School was legally registered and recognised. Support would sometimes manifest itself from unlikely quarters. When Christine Moffat took some photos of the area for the proposed school into the Ministry of Education, the official, looking at the hills in the background, quoted Psalm 121 unprompted:

> I lift up my eyes unto the hills —
> where does my help come from?
> My help comes from the LORD....

Christine found this enormously heartening.

## Notes

[1] In a note attached to a letter dated 10.01.04 from Jim Ford to the author. David and Marjorie Souter were missionaries from Dundee working in Kabwe. David is now a minister in the Church of Scotland in Perth.

[2] *Chengelo: The First Three Years*, p. 43.

[3] Mkushi Christian Fellowship Trust Co. Ltd. (MCFT Co. Ltd.) was registered as a private company within Section 5 of the Companies Acts with its Certificate of Incorporation 16353 dated 11.11.87. Chengelo Secondary School itself arose out of a Trust Deed dated 9.12.88 between MCFT Ltd and the Trustees (D Moffat, R Wyatt, B Young).

[4] Christine Moffat suspects that the buildings are now used for a basic school staffed by government teachers.

[5] Interview with author 16.05.04.

[6] Alfred Beit was a business associate of Cecil Rhodes who made his money in the diamond industry but had a reputation as a generous benefactor.

# Chapter Three

# The Pioneers

**The Opening of the School, 11th September 1988**
At 1400 on the 11th September 1988, Chengelo Secondary School opened its doors to its first pupils. 25 boys and 25 girls made up Forms 1 and 2. They became the Pioneers. There were similar numbers of Africans and Europeans, some three Indians and a small majority of mixed race.[1] After a gestation period of three years, in prayer, planning and preparation, Chengelo was born under an African sky.

Like all children going back to school, the first pupils arrived with a mixture of apprehension and expectation. They were met by houseparents who showed them to their hostels and their allocated beds. The boys were put into the converted farmhouse and the girls in the newly-built hostel. The school uniform was simple. It was white short-sleeve shirts, with navy skirts, short white socks and black leather shoes for girls. Boys wore white short-sleeve shirts, grey trousers, grey socks and black leather shoes. In the cold season a jacket could be worn with a grey jersey underneath. White tee shirts were worn for sport. In addition to their uniforms, pupils had been instructed to bring copies of the *Times of Zambia* and *Daily*

*Mail* for Friday 9th September, at least two magazines with coloured pictures, and any stamp collections. Girls were asked to bring sewing kits and patterns for the Sewing Club, and children could bring a poster to decorate their dormitory if they wished. As they unpacked they looked around curiously at the other pupils with whom they would live for the next four or five years.

### First Impressions

What were the first impressions of these new students? Natasha Arnold had visited the school for interview at the beginning of July. She travelled with two friends, Samantha Dale and Charlotte Rudy. It was a blazing hot day and the journey took much longer than necessary because the turning to the school was missed.

*All the way we talked about what we imagined the school would look like: lawns, flowerbeds, rose gardens, with only a few buildings as we knew it was a new school. The Headmaster would be a tall, stern, grey-haired man who always walked around with a cane in one hand and his Bible in the other! As we got closer and closer to the school, we saw nothing but bush apart from the Moffat and Wyatt farms and when we saw these we imagined Chengelo even more beautiful. We got out of the car onto the bare hard solid ground. There were no lawns or rose gardens in sight. What faced us was a little farm house and buildings —presumably classrooms, at the back which we only glanced at. A tiny fair-haired 'girl' walked out of the house and welcomed us to Chengelo.*

*'Good afternoon, I'm Mrs Solomon. My husband will be here in a minute. Would you like some cold drinks?' she said politely.*

*Sam, Charlotte and I looked at each other in amazement. And when we saw a slim, dark-haired man with a moustache, we sighed with relief. Mr Solomon showed us the half-built girls' hostel as we walked through the 'bush of a school', spare rooms in the old farmhouse, which were to be the boys' dormitories and so on. Truthfully, we were not impressed, but we were not discouraged because we felt a warm and caring atmosphere in our welcome to Chengelo.*

Natasha and her two friends were accepted for Chengelo. Natasha's account continues:

*On 11th September, 1988 – Opening day, I arrived late so missed the 'welcoming and thanksgiving' for the parents and students and all the new pupils had already settled in contently (sic). Things looked bright and beautiful as I had expected until supper was half an hour late and we had a not-so-delicious scrambled egg on toast. 'Oh no,' I thought, 'I hope not all the meals are going to be as disorganised as this.' A flash of home-sickness swept through me for a few seconds, and I began to wonder what it was that seemed so exciting that I wanted to leave my wonderful, luxurious home. I finally considered that this was Chengelo's opening day and things were bound to be not so perfect. Soon I settled in and got used to the disorganisation during the first week. A lot of unusual things happened during that first week, such as: two toilets breaking, a sink cracking in half, bathroom tiles collapsing due to disasters in the showers. This was all in the new girls' hostel. At the time, it seemed so depressing but when I look back at it, it was a totally hilarious week and one never to be forgotten.*

*Even though Chengelo didn't have any lawns, rose gardens or beautiful buildings, it held a warm family atmosphere and that is all that mattered. Mr and Mrs Solomon showed faith and willingness for the school and on the first day we knew Chengelo had a lot of exciting things in store for us.[2]*

Gradually the toilets were mended, meals served on time and Chengelo, like a young toddler, began to find its first feet. There was no tradition, no template, no precedent. Everything had to be worked out by trial and error, practice and prayer. So Chengelo like the cattle on the Moffats' farm grew on the hoof. But God had given the farmers a vision and three promises, and they trusted him to do what they felt was beyond their own expectations.

Every school has three basic requirements: pupils, teachers and facilities. How would the new Chengelo fare on these points?

## Admissions Policy

There was no shortage of applicants for the new school. There was something of a crisis in secondary education in Zambia in the late 1980s. State schools were starved of funds, and private schools were few and far between, having only belatedly been accepted by the Government. Indeed it was the weakness of secondary education which was driving both skilled expatriates and Zambian professionals out of the country. It was this need which had been one of the driving forces behind Chengelo's original vision. At the first meeting of the Board of Governors in November 1987, strict criteria were laid down concerning applicants. Admissions to the school were to be in accordance with the following priorities (with equal priority to the first three groups): the children of Mkushi farmers; the children of Christian workers who lived in rural areas and had problems with secondary education; the children of anyone living in a rural area where they had difficulty in finding suitable secondary education; the children of anyone else having difficulty with finding suitable secondary education, especially if of Christian parents.

Admissions would be at the discretion of the newly-formed Admissions Committee with no reasons being given. From the first the Governors were anxious to guard against nepotism, favouritism or undue pressure being used in the admissions process. The 50 places of the first pupils were well over-subscribed.

Finding staff was not quite so easy. The school was very blessed in the first three of the pioneering staff families, Neil and Ruby Solomon, David and Rachel Rust, and Keith and Barbara Rushby.

## Leading the School

The second couple on site were Neil and Ruby Solomon, who were to play such a pivotal role in establishing Chengelo on a firm foundation. Neil was educated at Hilton College and at Natal University in South Africa. It was whilst he was a pupil at Hilton that Michael Cassidy of African Enterprise conducted a mission in the school. During this mission Neil responded to God's call upon his life. In committing his life to Jesus Christ, Neil made a decision which would be determinative of much of what would happen to him over the next 27 years. At university Neil became an active member of the Mountain Club of South Africa. In 1979 Neil arrived at Treverton College to do his six weeks of practice teaching.

The third-term excursion took place during Neil's stay and Neil was appointed to lead an expedition in the Drakensburg Mountains. The party included the Headmaster, the Vice-Principal, another student teacher and seven Standard Eight schoolboys. The route recorded with the Parks Department was up the Organ Pipes Pass and down the nearby Tlanyaku Pass.

There was heavy snowfall and Neil hesitated about going further, but the two senior teachers urged him to press on. Tlanyaku Pass was found to be impassable with big drifts, so during a whole day the party traversed in atrocious conditions all the way to Greys Pass. At each resting place Neil would remove his pack and run to the top of the next hill to reconnoitre. On his return, without any rest for himself, he would lead the party onwards. After 12 hours of walking the party reached the bottom of Greys Pass by torchlight at 7 pm that night. There was no water at the campsite, so Neil, without hesitation, filled his rucksack with the empty bottles of the whole group and then headed downstream until he found water to bring back to the group.

Neil had clearly demonstrated his leadership qualities in a tricky situation, and it was no surprise when the

Headmaster appointed him an English teacher at Treverton for the following year.

During his time at Treverton Neil had shown himself to be in the words of Dr Alan Staples: 'Enterprising, adventurous, self-less, physically fit (well deserving of his Treverton nickname "Spring") caring, wise, thoughtful, superbly in touch with God's creation, exuberant for life. Dr Rex Mathie well recalls Neil's closing prayer at a Valedictory Service when he thanked God for the Umlambonja bum slide and the feel of mud oozing between one's toes.'[3] Neil had already shown himself to be a great ideas person with his running of the Treverton Post Matric Course and his book, *Reach Beyond*. During his time at Treverton, Neil met a certain dynamic biology teacher by the name of Ruby Stevens. They courted and got married and stole away for countless honeymoons in the mountains.

By the time of the Solomons' arrival at Chengelo they had two sons, Timothy and Luke, who took to their new life in Zambia like ducks to water. Neil and Ruby too revelled in their new life in Zambia. Neil hated apartheid and wrote to his parents of not wanting to go back to South Africa. It was only family and friends and the 'Berg' that drew him back. He said that he would definitely not return if the Conservatives came to power in South Africa. 'I could not bear the pangs of conscience I would feel walking the streets with a white skin, under the perverted laws that would result (not that they aren't totally sick and distorted already).'[4] He laughed at family and friends' concern for his safety in Zambia, when bombs were going off down south, and the biggest crime in Chengelo was the theft of a bag of mealie meal.

In January Neil wrote home: 'I'm feeling clean and fresh after a hot bath following a satisfying 7 km run with Neville Pietersen and one of the pupils.' Rachel Cook had arrived from England and with Florida Mutambo was taking the bulk of Neil's English lessons. 'I hardly have to teach now —just two lessons a week. This gives me the time to be a headmaster properly: Quite a few challenges this week: easing tensions that arose between two staff families, sorting out two pupils caught kissing in the library (two weeks of digging tree holes for an hour each day), plotting the course of a new drive which is being cleared through the trees, sitting through a 8 hour Board of Governors meeting ... it really is a varied and stimulating life.'[5]

Ruby wrote, 'I'm working really hard at my primary teaching and loving it! The children are responding so well too —I had one of them draw a picture the other day with "I like school" written in big letters across the top! Actually tonight Timothy and Luke went off to make a surprise and came back with a card saying "We like school" and pictures by them! ... The rain at this time of year is unbelievable —we haven't seen the sun for weeks and everywhere is mud and puddles!'[6] Shortly afterwards Neil wrote a newsletter to South Africa: 'As I sit here on the verandah, watching Timothy and Luke play on the lawn and looking beyond the fields to the hills, I realise afresh what an incredible opportunity we have been given. Professionally, I would struggle to find such a challenging and stimulating post anywhere else in the world. More important as a family, I can think of no better place to be living. ... The remoteness of Mkushi and the perennial problems of a Third World country are not everybody's cup of tea but, with the right attitude, they merely serve as spice to life. I really wish somebody would write a book about the amusing aspects of Third World living: Our latest shortage is matches and toilet paper.'[7]

## Teaching the Children

Visitors and new staff were sometimes surprised by the amount of noise and exuberant talking coming from one of the classrooms. They were told, 'It's just David – pupils don't fall asleep in his classes.' David Rust had had experience of working in Uganda and Kenya, as well as at

Oak Hill, a Christian school in Bristol, before taking up his post as Head of Humanities at Chengelo. Rachel Rust, who had also worked in Kenya, headed the Maths department. Rachel and David were the first houseparents of the girls' hostel. Their first impressions of Zambia were that nearly everything was in short supply. Initially there was no wheat flour and then a dearth of cooking oil. But they had arrived at Chengelo and they shared its vision.

A week before the school opened David wrote home to say that he had been busy repairing and painting an old swimming pool. But the workers' houses, the laundry and ironing rooms and kitchen lean-to were still not built. The classrooms had still to be cleared of stores. Most worryingly the airfreight with all the Rusts' teaching resources had not yet arrived. In the frantic period leading up to and going on from the 11th of September, Chengelo's opening day, there was not much time for letter writing. On the evening of the 4th October by the light of a candle, David wrote to his parents saying:

*I've never been so hectic in all my life. We moved into the hostel on the Friday and tried to get ourselves sorted out as best we could in the home and get the school set up before the children arrived on Sunday. We had an open air thanksgiving service on the Sunday morning. The first week was good but it seemed interminable with everything new and no routine established. The children were rather all over the place and needed sitting on in the first few days. Now it's the 4th week they know what's expected of them, but it really took a full 2 weeks to get firm boundaries established; and of course now we are working on establishing our expectations for smaller things like homework in on time etc.*

*Life is exciting here – never a dull moment – it's like one huge family. We do not yet have a school caterer. Anne Wyatt and Yvonne Young have taken it on and are doing a fantastic job – the children are amazed at the quantity and quality – they always have more than enough to eat....*

*The swimming pool here is operational though quite*

*muddy as the water comes from the stream and we have no filter. By the start of term I had worked with a gang of labourers and levelled and marked out 2 badminton courts, 2 volleyball courts, 1 netball court, so with that and space for rounders and football, and a strong emphasis on cross-country running we all keep pretty fit....*

*We believe that God is wanting Chengelo to be the best school in Zambia.... There is such excitement about the school, and news of it is spreading like wildfire by word of mouth in government circles, the churches, the business community etc.... At times it seems an awesome responsibility but God has given the vision so clearly and miraculously provided funds, people and resources, again and again.*

As the term moved from September to October the weather got hotter and more oppressive. Then came merciful relief. 'The rains have just started and it's beautifully refreshing. It was becoming unbearably hot and sticky.... We have had enormous cloud bursts in the last few days.... We wake now to the beautiful scent of the gums. The pink and crimson bougainvillaeas are in full bloom and the brilliant mauve jacaranda trees are just beginning to shed their petals.... There have been plenty of bush fires.... Often at night we have had huge fires nearby.'

Chengelo provided the opportunity to see agriculture in practice. One day David Rust took the children on a farm visit to see a dam under construction, to watch cattle dipping, a field being ploughed for maize and another where coffee seedlings were being transplanted. But David also made time for fun. As he wrote home,

*Two weekends ago I took them all down to the river after breakfast on a Sunday morning and we had organised mud fights in teams which was great and then on to a deep pool where we swam in the fast flowing current among the water lilies, to wash all the mud off. There is a great debate about whether we should swim in the river because there is a*

*small risk of bilharzia and a minute risk of crocodiles. We*
*are of course being very sensible in taking every available*
*precaution – don't worry.*[8]

In a short space of time the Rusts were having to get used to an invasion of large flying ants, and a huge tarantula which made his nest in a hole about three metres from one of the classrooms. During the day he spun his web over the hole, but at night he sat on the top of his hole waiting for his prey. They had a couple of tiny tree frogs with beautiful red stripes living on the back door. More fearful was a spitting cobra, which got into the school pantry. There was also an enormous python, which wrapped itself around a three-week old calf and killed it. Russell Wyatt shot the python and brought it into school.[9] It was measured at 3.6 metres. The boys had great delight in skinning it preparatory to hanging up the skin as a trophy in their new hostel.

## Shopping for Chengelo

The Rushbys had been the first of the expatriate staff to arrive. Keith's job description was defined tongue-in-cheek by David Moffat as Administrative Expediter. Barbara, who was a trained bookkeeper and secretary, arrived with her portable typewriter, and acted as the school secretary before being drawn into the accounts. The Rushbys came at Russell Wyatt's invitation for a flexible period of three months to three years. In the event they stayed nearly thirteen years, and gave the school the benefit of continuity as well as their maturity and life experience. They had been given a prophecy by Arthur Wallis, one of the leaders of their Cornerstone Church, that God had something for them to do which would fit them like a glove fits the hand. This proved to be the case. After staying with the Wyatts and the Moffats, the Rushbys moved into the farm manager's guest cottage, which consisted of a bedroom, lounge and kitchen.

Keith put his hand to everything at first, but then he

devoted himself to looking after the stores and doing the shopping. He shopped initially for building supplies and then for the school food and stationery. A shopping trip was a major expedition. The school had been given a double-cab pickup for Keith to use. The problem was that the van had no effective brakes, the steering was uneven, a rear window was boarded over, the driver's window of perspex needed two hands to raise it and the van had no heating.

Police roadblocks were common. After leaving one it was difficult to drive in a straight line as two hands were needed to raise the driver's window. Policemen would often ask Keith with his impressive beard if he was the Headmaster. He would say, 'I have got a much more important job than that. I do the shopping!' The police would agree with that.

On the cold winter mornings in which they first began shopping trips, Barbara would wear a tracksuit and wrap herself in a blanket. At first the trips were to Lusaka. It would take about four hours to reach it, a journey of some 320 kms. The start would be in the dark at 4 am, returning by about 8 pm. Some time later a rule was made that there should be no driving of school vehicles after dark because of the risk of accident, particularly from running into unlit vehicles.

After a while Barton Young bought a new single-cab for Chengelo, with a canopy to protect the shopping. Later still a delivery van was purchased because the shopping was enclosed with the driver and guard and therefore much easier to look after.

As the school grew, so did the supplies required. Most of the shopping was then done in Ndola on the Copperbelt, which is about an hour nearer the school. For a while one-day trips sufficed, but later the Rushbys worked out a routine whereby they stayed the night. They would go round the first day ordering the supplies. On the morning of the second day, they would go round again and pay for the goods and a lorry would come from the school to carry the bulk of them. Barbara would sit for most of the two days in the van, guarding the cash and any small items not going into the lorry. She was armed only with a whistle, which she found an effective deterrent on the two occasions that she used it. She also learnt never to turn her back on an open window or allow herself to be distracted. She would keep Keith supplied with drinks and record the cash as it was spent. Some suppliers had secure parking but most did not. Keith shopped for most things, but Barbara bought for the school tuck shop and then sometime Keith had to guard the van.

In the early days the Rushbys discovered that it was one thing to shop for supplies. It was another thing to find any available. Their first visit to a supermarket in Ndola found a full shop, but all the shelves were mainly loaded with just four items: toilet rolls, Lifebuoy soap, Colgate toothpaste and Cobra polish. Getting flour could be a major problem. They would go to the mill in Kabwe. It took the best part of the morning to obtain a piece of paper from the friendly manager, which allowed them to pick up flour from the mill. Then it took all afternoon to get the flour from the mill and loaded into the pickup. Later most things became available, though with limited choice. It helped when goods began to come into the shops from South Africa.

On one occasion they were using a pickup without a canopy. Keith had three big cartons of cereals on the back and then loaded 24 cases of syrup (480 jars in all). Barbara watched while the syrup was put on, covered with a tarpaulin, and then securely lashed down by Keith. As Keith drove off, she got in. After they got back to Chengelo Keith commented that he was a case of syrup short. The next morning there was a phone call to the school from Jayhinds, a wholesaler in Ndola, asking whether they had got all their supplies. Barbara said that there was a case of syrup short and Jayhinds said they had it. They had seen someone going down the road with a case of syrup carried on his head. They thought it strange because only they sold syrup. They chased after him, whereupon he put the syrup down and ran off. It was a complete mystery how the syrup was stolen from the pickup when such care had been taken.

With devaluation and inflation, a briefcase was needed to carry all the cash. But as the school became known, Chengelo was one of the few customers who would readily have their cheques accepted. The school was trusted and never bounced a cheque. But even so towards the end of their time they were carrying up to four million kwacha in cash as well as paying by cheque. When they first arrived in Zambia the exchange rate was K12 – K15 to £1. When they left in 2001 it was around K7,000 to £1.

## Keeping the Accounts

Barbara Rushby kept the school accounts with great conscientiousness. She was helped after a time by Florida Mutambo, who transferred to the accounts department from the teaching staff. As the school grew so did the amount of accounts work and it got very behind. Keith and Barbara purchased a computer accounts package in the UK. Keith installed it but they found that it could not cope with the number of kwacha involved. Keith then purchased a much more sophisticated accounts package. This was installed by Rami Ghali, a chartered accountant, who came out from Bristol to help for one year. He was invaluable and worked hard to bring the accounts up to date and put in some excellent systems. Rami's great virtues included a really caring nature. 'He would always look out for people on their own and make sure that they were alright.'[10] Barbara was also helped by three wives of other staff, Maureen Mazyopa, Niya Musonda and Jean Lungu. Together they formed a great team.

Communications between expatriates and locals could easily be subject to misunderstanding. Barbara remembers an incident with her gardener. One day she asked him to remove the rose leaves affected by black spot. When she returned she discovered that the gardener had removed not only the damaged leaves but all the leaves, so that the roses stood naked on their bare stems. [11] Generally the bush telegraph ensured that the locals knew all about their 'basungu' (Europeans). This is why the delightful house girl who worked for the Rushbys was so thunderstruck when they told her that they were moving house and she did not already know anything about it!

Florida Mutambo (née Kusaloka), who helped Barbara with the accounts, had originally come to Mkushi in September 1983 to work with Stanbic Bank. She began worshipping with the Mkushi Christian Fellowship. She then met her husband Neston Mutambo, a former chairman of the University Christian Fellowship, who had come to Mkushi as cattle manager for Glenys Kingdom, a local farmer. Neston and Florida were married in November 1986 and became regular members of the Fellowship. Florida was present at the October 1985 retreat when Gordon Suckling was the speaker and had joined in the discussions about the proposed school. When Chengelo opened in September 1988, Florida began to teach English, initially for one day a week. Later she agreed to teach three days a week and would stay overnight with Anne Carrington, the Headmaster's secretary, for this period. Florida's daughter Luwi was born in October 1987, and she has three other children, Wezi, Tozya and Wani. Neston started farming on his own account, but later worked as an extension officer with a cotton outreach team. For the last few years he has worked with Trinity Broadcasting Network, a Christian broadcasting station in Zambia.

**Reinforcing the Staff**
John Ngulube was one of the first Zambian members of staff, and joined Chengelo in November 1989. John read Mathematics at the University of Zambia, and was an active

member of the Christian Union. In addition to teaching Maths, John enjoyed coaching football and leading discipleship groups and the Sunday evening worship. On 31st August 1991, John married Mwaka Chabatama at Mpika. It was described as 'a day of joy and celebration concluding two years of romance and the beginning of a new chapter in their lives together.'[12] John is still teaching at Chengelo. But as we have seen the accolade of the first Zambian staff member must go to Florida Mutambo, who in addition to being a busy wife and mother, travelled up to Chengelo on a Monday, taught English on Tuesdays, Wednesdays and Thursdays, and then returned home on Fridays. Mrs Mutambo is still on the staff working as an accountant.

The initial staff was supplemented in November 1988 by Keith and Gita George, who arrived at Chengelo with their son, Simon, and a dog, Sandy. Keith George taught Geography, but mapwork was his passion and his students spent much time plotting farms or studying contours on a hill. Gita George acted as the school nurse and tended many pupils through chickenpox, malaria and flu. She also helped with the school accounts when Barbara Rushby was away. After a year at Chengelo, the Georges moved on to work at Mpongwe Mission, with its hospital, in Luanshya. Gita's work as nurse was taken over by Robyn Mahaffey, whose husband, Mike, was part of the MMM team who had finished the first hostel in time for the school to open. Mike now took charge of the building work. In September 1989 Mike and Beverley Robinson, another couple from the Bristol Christian Fellowship, together with their two teenage children, Simon and Katie, joined the staff. Mike Robinson had spent two years in the Royal Marines and then worked in the advertising business. Beverley had been a model, a hotel manager, freelance seller and stable hand. Both the Robinsons got involved at Chengelo in physical education, Bible study and discipleship groups, and counselling pupils. Mike became the rugby coach and Beverley helped out with horse-riding and stable management. They also ran a first aid clinic after Robyn Mahaffey left.

One year after the Robinsons, Ian and Alison Richardson, also from Bristol, arrived at Chengelo. Ian, who had a degree in chemistry, became Head of Science, and Alison taught the school for junior staff children. Evan and Kabaenda Mbozi joined the staff in September 1990 having previously taught at Matero Girls School in Lusaka. Mr Mbozi taught French and English, was a keen astronomer and coached the football team to several victories. Mrs Mbozi helped Alison Richardson with the primary children and taught some Geography in the secondary school.

**Feeding the School**

One of the most urgent needs of the new school was to find a caterer. Whilst the school awaited the arrival of Doreen Brown, who could not join Chengelo until September 1989, Anne Wyatt nobly filled the gap. She fed the school for most of the first year from the small farmhouse kitchen. It consisted of one wood-burning stove and two gas stoves. It was staffed by five men and Aunty Anne, as Anne Wyatt became universally known. Her right hand man was Special Ntambu, a first class and experienced cook of the old style. The Headmaster paid this tribute: 'We do want to single one person out and that is our beloved 'Aunty Anne Wyatt', who through her unflagging efforts has kept our catering department running smoothly. In the opinion of the writer (who has had some 20 years first-hand experience of boarding schools) the Chengelo food beats them all.'[13] The little lounge in the farmhouse had to accommodate fifty people in one room. To prevent pushing and shoving the pupils were instructed to stand in line at one arm's length apart before collecting their food from the service table next to the kitchen hatch.

Russell Wyatt says, 'For the first year we used one steer a term, and I did all the butchery for two or three years.

It was great fun. We did it at home and then when we had facilities we moved up here to the school. I was a butcher and a builder.'

Doreen Brown stayed for one year and was followed as caterer by Helen Jack, a farmer's daughter from Suffolk and then Lisa Davenport from Bath in England. Anne Wyatt took over in the gaps between the comings and goings, and generally oversaw and managed the domestic staff and the laundry as she still does till the present time.

## Building Chengelo

The original buildings that stood on the Chengelo site consisted of Lilanda, the old farmhouse built by Robert Moffat, and a two-bedroom annex that the Moffats lived in before Lilanda was built. In addition there was a manager's house with one bedroom, lounge, bathroom and kitchen (which had originally been stables), and the manager's guest cottage consisting of one bedroom and a bathroom. The first alterations were to make Lilanda and its annex suitable for a boys' hostel, with the lounge becoming the first dining room. The manager's house was the home for the Solomons, with the addition of two bedrooms and the bricking-in of the verandah to give access to the new bedrooms. The guest cottage was extended to make a lounge and a kitchen. This was the first home for the Rushbys. The remaining buildings were the prefabricated classrooms acquired for the school from the mines by Jim Ford.

The first entirely new building was the girls' hostel with twelve dormitories and bathrooms. Russell Wyatt supervised the laying of the foundations and the early building of this hostel. He was assisted by Keith Rushby, and they used farm labour and the embryonic school building team, which consisted of Hosea, Patson and Kennedy. David Souter came up from time to time and loaned a concrete mixer, as well as a bricklayer and a helper. By July the hostel was up to roof level, when

Russell and Anne Wyatt went on overseas leave. At this juncture, the Australians of MMM arrived to put on the roof and complete the building.[14] Two common rooms were built on one wing, and a staff flat was attached to the hostel. The girls were able to move in to the hostel for the first day of term.

From the first Chengelo was a building site. Russell Wyatt remembers those early days.[15]

*I looked after the building, David Moffat the finances and purchases, and Barton Young the grounds and sports fields. I remember standing with David and Christine somewhere near the present library, and of course there was nothing then, and said, 'Do you really want a school, which might become a big school, right in the middle of your farm?' They thought about it and they said, 'Yes'. It was their decision. We have never had to stop work because of lack of money. We went away one April on holiday overseas, and talking with David we could see that we would have to close down at the end of April if more funding did not come in. And David phoned me in England and said that we would not have to close down. That was the closest that we came to stopping work. Apart from one or two work stoppages, which probably lasted no more than a day or two, we have built something every day from the day that work started, which I think was the 24th March 1988. We started laying the foundations of the girls' junior hostel and the girls moved in in early September.*

In Year 2 the school faced a 100% increase in the number of pupils as the school expanded from 50 to 100 students. The priority was to build the boys' hostel so that the boys could move out of Lilanda and its annex. The second priority was the construction of the dining-hall and kitchen, with its stores, butchery and washing-up facilities. The dining room was finished in time for the marriage of Andy Patching and Eira, Gordon and Peggy Suckling's daughter and the sister of Anne Bentley. These were followed by the first of the detached staff houses for the Robinsons and the Rusts. At the same time the space between classroom 1 and the office was covered in to make separate offices for the Headmaster and his secretary. A further influx of 50 new pupils in January 1991 necessitated the building of more student hostels. Two wings of new hostels were put up, one for senior girls and the other for junior boys. It was intended to complete the second wing of each hostel in time for the following year. Next a clinic with ten beds was built, with a house attached to accommodate the Mahaffeys, Mrs Mahaffey being the school nurse. This clinic replaced an old caravan which had stood behind the girls' hostel.

Another caravan was used by Keith and Barbara Rushby for administration and accounts. It also contained the radio, linking the school to the local farmers' network. At this stage the school had no telephone. Until Chengelo was connected to the national telephone system, Michelle Cantlay played a key role in passing phone messages to and from the school. Before the school was connected by satellite to the internet, Michelle, who taught computing at Chengelo, also managed the e-mail system from her home.

A further intake of 50 pupils in January 1992 meant that the two unfinished hostels required the completion of their second wings, although the Form 5 wing for girls and the boys' common room were not finished on time. Four new classrooms had to be built for English, French, Art and Geography. The classrooms were built with Chengelo's own home-made cement blocks and fire-baked bricks. From a site behind the foundations of the new classrooms, a large area was cleared around an anthill. The anthill was dug out and clay was mixed with water to make a sticky mud mix, which was put into moulds and then left to dry in the sun. After a few weeks the bricks were stacked to form a kiln and coated with mud. Then a fire was lit within the kiln. The fire was kept going 24 hours a day for one whole week. These bricks were also used to build a new staff house for the Bentleys. Brian Bentley was to join the staff as the administrator. Chengelo was rising from the bush.

**Notes**
[1] Today the overwhelming majority of students are Africans.
[2] *Chengelo: The First Three Years* edited by Anne D Carrington, p. 52.
[3] A Tribute by Dr Alan Staples at Neil's funeral.
[4] Letter from Neil to parents dated 20.09.88.
[5] Letter from Neil to parents dated 23.01.89.
[6] Letter from Ruby dated 03.02.89.
[7] Newsletter from Neil dated February 1989.
[8] Letter to the family from David Rust dated 20.10.88.
[9] The python is now a protected species in Zambia.
[10] Interview with author on 14.04.04.
[11] This is not an uncommon problem even with Zambians. Mrs Leah Mutala reports that her flower garden has been razed again and again.
[12] Op. cit., p. 28.
[13] *Chengelo Newsletter: First Term 1988.*
[14] Information supplied by Christine Moffat with Russell Wyatt's notes sent by e-mail dated 06.05.05.
[15] Interview with author on 17.05.04.

# Chapter Four

# The Early Years

The School Song

Chorus
*Oh Chengelo, as a witness to the light*
*Of our Saviour Jesus Christ*
*May His name be forever glorified*
*May His name be forever glorified*
*In this place.*

Rising from the soil of Zambia
Chengelo was built by faith
God gave a vision of a beacon on a hill
Let His light shine through us still.
*Chorus*

We are proud to bear the name, Chengelo
We strive for His best in every way
Out on the sportsfield, the classroom or hill
Does His light shine through us still?

The school song was composed by Ruby Solomon and expressed all that Chengelo stood for. Now that the school was up and running, it was the responsibility of governors, staff and pupils to ensure that the light of Christ shone out on the sportsfield, classroom and hill. But this could be no 'head in the clouds' experience, for the situation on the ground was far from visionary.

## The Rains

After the heat of October, the first two years brought rain in abundance, and with the rain came the mud. Vangela Dakis describes the mud. 'The rains of '89 were the worst Chengelo has ever come across. They started in early November and poured until late March. We were well into term 1 when the floods came. This made commuting between hostel and classroom literally impossible for the mud, mud and more mud. We didn't have to walk far as our school consisted of a mere six buildings then, but we were up to our eyeballs in the stuff and terribly sick of it. ...Everyone, with hardly an exception, lived in gumboots, raincoats and umbrellas. Our motto that term was "survival of the very wet!" In those days we had no white sand or sophisticated paving stones there are now. If you put your foot in the mud, you either stayed there till a crane came to haul you out, or you amputated your foot. Yes, life was tough then!'[1] The rains were so heavy that at one time all the roads into the school had to be closed off as even the tractors were getting stuck in the mud. The laundry was stretched to the limit, and it was not uncommon to enter the kitchen at night and find line upon line of drying socks and underwear.

Neil Solomon decided that the rains would be an ideal time to initiate the boys of Forms 1 and 2 in some camping experience. Camp was established some three or four kilometres from the school. The boys were divided into two groups and told to make a tarpaulin shelter. The evening was spent in laying traps for the other group and in wrestling with Paul and Phil Ravenstein, two Australian builders from Mobile Mission Maintenance (MMM) who accompanied the party. About midnight the heavens opened and the nearby stream rose metres and flooded Mr Solomon's tent. After dragging himself through hip-high water, he found himself wandering blindly into the war zone of the two camps and began to fall one by one into the various traps laid for intruders. He found his boys enjoying a newly invented game of 'fanta, fanta, orange, fanta.' It was then sludge all the way back to school through the rains and the mud.

The heavy rains impeded the building work. However with the help of the two Ravenstein brothers of MMM, the roofing timbers for the new boys' hostel were in place by the end of February 1989, and 25 boys were able to move into one wing of the hostel by the middle of the year. Lighting equipment imported from the UK was now installed and being connected up. Neville Pietersen from Bristol had taken charge of the building and maintenance work, and by July 1989 the dining and kitchen block was up to roof height. This and two new staff houses were needed for the new school year. But the 60% devaluation of Zambian currency, together with a similar rise in wages and the total decontrol of prices, had increased costs dramatically, and the basic building expenses for wages and cement had doubled.

## Entertainment

The school made great efforts to build bridges with the local farming community, which was generally most supportive and generous in its giving. The Food Science group had several dinners for staff and farmers from around the Mkushi Farm Block. These were largely set up by Michelle Cantlay, who taught Food Science. The first dinner consisted of chicken tandoori and vegetable salad, followed by different coloured meringues with strawberries and ice cream, fruit salad in a watermelon basket, and chocolate cake. The tables were decorated with white tablecloths, flowers and candles. Punch was served during the evening, and the French group sang songs and performed a dance and a play. On another occasion the Food Science group presented a Chinese meal. The farmers reciprocated by inviting the pupils to the Mkushi Country Club for games.

The end of the first academic year was celebrated with a 'Pioneers' Ball', in which all the pupils dressed up in weird and wonderful costumes ranging from Madonna to Rod Stewart, with Sacha Fertig from Form 1 dressing as Mr Solomon, and Mr Solomon dressing as Sacha Fertig.

The first prize giving was held on 28th July 1989. The guest speaker was Dr Gunnar Holmgren, from a well-known missionary family. Christine Moffat, Anne Wyatt and Yvonne Young handed out the prizes.

The school doubled in size in September 1989. Neil Solomon reported in November 1989: 'This term has been quite a difficult one, but not without a sense of deep satisfaction. It took a few weeks to establish the 50 new pupils and, for a while, our facilities were stretched to cope with a doubled enrolment. Ill health took its toll with 25 cases of chickenpox and various viral infections that at one stage had 20% of the pupils in bed. The satisfaction came from the strength God has given us to cope, and in seeing many pupils responding to His message of salvation. It has also been rewarding to hear the positive comments from our farming community regarding the helpful behaviour and manners of Chengelo children.'[2]

Norma Grenzenberg, a former Treverton colleague, whom the Solomons happened to bump into on the London Underground, was now teaching in the staff primary school, thus releasing Ruby Solomon to teach Biology and Music at the secondary school. Grindlays Bank International had also come up with financial assistance for the building of the dining-hall, which was now receiving its finishing touches. One of the first events put on in the new dining-hall was a party to mark the end of 1989. Natasha Arnold wrote that the dining-hall was decorated with streamers, balloons and posters, and more food than they had ever before seen at Chengelo. 'At first, everyone was shy to dance and it took a while for the young gentlemen to pluck up enough courage to ask the young ladies to dance. The DJs of the night did a wonderful job of playing different kinds of music to suit everybody's taste. But by the time people started enjoying themselves, it was time for the party to end and everyone was disappointed. The generator was switched off at 23.00 hours (not the usual time of 22.00 hours) and everyone went to bed.'[3]

### School Routine

So Chengelo started to settle down to the school routine. This daily routine[4] began at 06.00 in the morning with wake-up and wash, the making of beds and tidying of the dormitories. At 06.15 there was a quiet time for Bible reading, journal writing or thinking. During the hot season morning sports followed at 06.30 to avoid the heat of the day. The school was 'suddenly alive with figures in white shorts and shirts as they run towards the sports field in groups to play netball, soccer, touch rugby, flingelo (a game played between two teams with a frisbee) or softball. A few people wander around with bundles of sticks to make a fire in three minutes and others with shovels and bricks do something for "community service". Then by 07.30 everyone is already weaving their way back to the hostels or running to shower in time for breakfast.'[5] A breakfast of mealie meal porridge, toast and hot tea followed at 08.00.

Every weekday the school gathered for morning assembly. This took place collectively in the dining-hall, or separately in individual classrooms. There were generally notices, a talk by a staff member or visitor, and a prayer. Lessons followed morning assembly and these were interrupted at 10.15 with a tea break. Pupils rushed out of the classroom and up to the dining hall in order to be first in line for tea and sandwiches (either tomato, egg, cheese, fish, corned beef or jam). The staff walked to their common room for tea or coffee, sandwiches, biscuits and cakes. 'At 12.30 every weekday, Chengelo takes a deep breath from the business of the morning. School books are put aside, reading books and novels are brought out.... Sustained Undisturbed Reading for Enjoyment (S.U.R.E.)[6] has begun. You then witness a time when the school clock stands still. Everyone – pupils, teachers and headmaster – all become absorbed in the pages of a good book. All heads are bent low, the only sound is the sound of pages being turned. The still and silent (*sic*) lasts a mere 30 minutes. When the bell rings again, life bursts back to normal. Briefcases fly to their owners, books are clutched to the chests and the race to the dining hall for lunch is on.'[7]

After lunch there was an hour's siesta before the school came back to life for afternoon classes. David Domingo wrote, 'As the day closes and the sun begins to set, the bell rings and pupils start getting into line for the last meal of the day. "What are we having tonight?" they all ask. They sit and wait patiently and think about what has been done that day.... As they bite into their food, their faces brighten with the satisfaction of having French toast and salad to finish. The pupils never forget to give thanks to the Provider and remember to be thankful to the cooks who prepare the meals.'[8] After supper came homework or prep for one-and-a-half hours with a five-minute break in the middle. There was a short time of free time before lights out, when there was time to wash socks and underclothes and get books ready for the next day. Lights out was at 20.45 for Form 1's, and 21.30 for Form 4.

## Weekends

There was a different routine for weekends. There could be a run before breakfast, which was followed by the inspection of the dormitories by one of the teachers. Marks were awarded from 1 to 10, with 8 and above being excellent, 7 good, 6 fair and 5 and below counting as a fail. At the end of the term marks were added up for each dormitory and the dorm with the most marks received a treat, such as coffee and pancakes at a staff house, or going to the Kingdoms' dam for windsurfing. Because some of the boys were very untidy, daily inspections were introduced to keep them up to scratch. Lessons and prep for the senior forms were a regular feature of Saturday mornings with games in the afternoons. A video such as a comedy or a documentary was often shown on a Saturday evening. Pupils were allowed a lie-in until about 07.45 on a Sunday. They generally enjoyed free time on Sundays, but all pupils were expected to write a Sunday letter home each week. Sunday lunches were special with roast beef or pork or chicken with potatoes and vegetables, followed by a tasty pudding. The passport for Sunday lunch was to produce a finished letter. Lombe Malama confessed that some pupils had even gone to the lengths of sending a blank piece of paper in their addressed and stamped envelope.

On Sunday evenings there was, and still is, a voluntary church service for the pupils. Sharyn Edwards felt that Chengelo had something, which was missing in many boarding schools in the first world. 'Education, self-discipline, physical ambition and continuous spiritual development is the recipe for the success at Chengelo, which is why you will find that most people have a composed and self-assured attitude to life. Part of this is owed to the famous Chengelo celebrations; not 'mass' or service but celebration. We used to call them 'church services', like everybody else, but then we realised that we needed to do much more than gather in a room and sit it out while a staff member quotes a dozen verses from the Bible. Sunday nights are spent in dedication to God; praising Him, thanking Him and sometimes crying for Him.'[9] On one Sunday a term the Mkushi Christian Fellowship have a combined service with the school in the dining-hall.

Pupils are allowed home on certain weekends during the year. And there are weekend excursions. Esther Kamata described a night's camping for seven girls at the Youngs' farm during one half-term break. On arrival, 'the little group had an interesting experience picking Himalayan berries. Despite millions of thorns and awkward bushes, the girls had a great time with evidence of purple stains over their mouths. More went in their mouths than in the pot! Setting up camp was a chaotic event —seven girls and four unpitched tents don't really associate! ...Supper was well on the way by then, but only served at 20.40. Mrs Young, better known as Aunty Yvonne, had doughnuts, hot-cross buns and coffee ready for us all after that... while the inaugural speech of the new president on that day, President Chiluba, kept our attention. A game of squash and a swim at 23.30, instead of sending us to sleep, woke us all up. The late night did not stop the girls having fun the next morning. Up at 06.00, breakfast on the plough disc, then an enthusiastic group set off into the orchard to peaches, apples and nectarines, the girls thought they were clever as they found a new routine, one for the basket, one for the mouth! A very, very enjoyable outing was had by all which couldn't really be called 'camping' but playing squash, swimming, watching TV, etc., but I'm sure none of the girls want to see another peach again! (until next year anyway!)'[10]

## Discipline

At first the school had no regulated system of punishments. Lombe Malama described how this developed.[11]

*Pupils were punished according to what a member of staff felt was suitable for them. This was at times unfair. Pupils were getting punished differently for the same offence. This was the case in 1990 when three Form 3s, Hans, Titus and Fred, were not allowed to send laundry for a week because their dorm was in such a tip. This punishment was given by Mr Solomon. One term later the same offence was committed by two other Form 3s, Chembe and Sacha. This time Mr Robinson gave them dried cow dung nailed to a plank and told them to keep it in the dorm for three days.*

*For the past two years Chengelo has had some strange and unusual punishments. For instance, the 'Welly Boot Run' for boys only. They were dragged out of their beds on a Saturday morning and told to run a certain number of times around the sports field. They were only to wear their swimming trunks and Wellington boots. Some of the other unusual punishments were: waking up at 06.00 and standing outside the headmaster's office, and counting trees.*

*This continued until sometime in 1990 when Mr Robinson came up with an idea: a person would be given a piece of paper and the offence committed would be written on it. At the end of term, all the debits were to be counted for each person and the total would be written on their reports. The staff agreed and it was called 'The Debit System....'*

*This system worked for three months and then stopped having an effect on pupils as they saw it as only a piece of paper. The staff met again to make the system work more effectively. It was decided that each debit would carry a number of minutes (detention) depending on the severity of the offence....*

*Then on Wednesday, which is a free afternoon, pupils had to do manual work equivalent to the number of minutes (detention).... It also means that anyone on detention has to wear uniform all day Wednesday, and miss tuck shop that week. This system has become more effective so it has stayed ever since, with some adjustments every now and again. For example, to reward good behaviour, credits are given.*

A more elaborate system known as responsibility ratings was introduced into the school in Term 1 1991. Those who showed responsibility were rewarded with certain privileges. The highest grade A was given to those who proved themselves reliable and trustworthy, and showed compassion, sensitivity and integrity. A Graders might stay up after dorm lights out, watch a video on Wednesday night, shower at any time and keep tuck. The gradings were assessed by the staff on a fortnightly basis. The girls in the senior hostel brought in a highly sophisticated system of spots and dots. Each pupil started the week with five coloured spots and dots. Any misbehaviour, such as leaving clothes in the washroom, would forfeit a dot or spot. Pink cards were awarded for four or five spots or dots remaining at the end of each week. Five pink cards could be exchanged for a blue card. A blue card carried certain rewards, such as a bar of chocolate or a cake, and five blue cards earned a day at the Youngs' farm.

A further development was the setting up of the Student Representative Council which first met in 1991. The membership was made up of A and B Graders. The Headmaster oversaw the elections, which resulted in Bupe Pihlblad being elected as chairman and Sharyn Edwards as secretary. Committees were formed to handle issues concerning the hostels, food, dining-hall and kitchen, sports and evening activities. Any pupil could raise a problem with an SRC member who would ask the secretary to include the matter on the next agenda. Early success for the SRC was in the provision of juice and biscuits for Saturday break, and coffee for top forms after Saturday video. But the exercise of democracy produced a certain disillusionment, and it was reported that some members had walked out of the Council.

## Rust Correspondence

David and Rachel Rust continued with their correspondence home. They reported that one weekend they entertained some Zambian friends, Isaac and Betty, and Neston and Florida. Neston Mutambo was manager of the farm next to the Moffats. Isaac got advice from Neston and Russell on buying a farm in the district.

'On Thursday David was meant to take some children over to Barton's farm for the life-skills lesson on agriculture. Unfortunately he got delayed in Lusaka, so a message was radioed through. (The radios each farm have are invaluable —everybody has one, and as it's a C. B. one, we all hear each others news!) So instead David Moffat took them as the vet was up doing Pregnancy Diagnosis on the cattle. The children came back so excited, having spent the afternoon with their arms up cows' backsides, feeling in the womb for the baby foetus.'[12]

Rachel Rust had to go home for a rest in 1989 not having properly picked up after malaria and general stress. In July 1989 David Rust was writing home to say that Chengelo was 'like a little oasis of peace in a troubled land. Poor Zambia is rather chaotic at present. The kwacha was devalued by 60%, just before Rachel left for England. It had already been devalued by 20% a few months earlier.... All price controls were lifted at the same time as the devaluation, so prices rocketed this month.... The man who stokes our fires just couldn't cut the wood properly yesterday. He and his family have run out of food for the month – they only have mealie meal left – nothing to go with it; pay day is meant to be this week, so I helped him with K10 – but that doesn't stretch at all. Now there is real chaos in the country. We suddenly had an announcement on Saturday, with no notice at all, that all currency was being changed. Everyone has to get to a bank before Aug. 3rd to exchange their bank notes for the new currency. We can only exchange K2000 at a time. No one can change more than a total of K10,000 without explaining why they have so much. The whole process is to crack the currency-dealing on the black market.... One friend of the Wyatts' went into the bank yesterday at 8am to change money, and came out at 12.30, still not having been served because of the queues.'[13]

Two months later, David wrote to say that with double the number of pupils in the school, 'We've been stretched till we thought that we couldn't be stretched any more, and then things have become even more busy, but we've survived....' Work was proceeding on the dining-room and the timbers were sent to the wood-drying kiln. But then the President's Office decreed that all timber in the kiln should go elsewhere. This meant that there was no roof for the dining-room and meals were served under an open sky. But this proved a blessing in disguise because it was discovered that the metal supports for the rafters had been put in upside down. Three Australians were coming to fix the roof.

A very insensitive racial comment by one girl had caused uproar in the hostel. 'It was a good time the other night to face up to the hurts and begin to ask for God's healing in many lives. We believe that as children begin to learn to live in harmony here and bring God into hurts and problems, people will see Chengelo as "A Witness to the Light" which is the school motto.'[14] David Rust still found time in the midst of everything else to organise a 'Mastermind Competition'. Students were given two weeks to prepare for the quiz. Half the questions were chosen from a Bible book of their choice, and half were general knowledge. The finalists were Annette Cowham and George Nicoll. Eventually Annette was declared the winner. [15]

By the end of 1990 Chengelo had expanded to a staff of 22 and students were coming from Lusaka and the Copperbelt and all over Zambia, with some taking up to eleven hours to reach the school. The Rusts settled down to their third really hot Christmas. Rebecca Rust wrote to her grandparents, 'It rains nearly every day, and there are so many flies that they wake you up in the morning by crawling all over your face. This morning I was swatting the flies with the fly swat, when it broke because I hit a fly really hard! A few weeks ago we went camping at the Youngs' dam. We didn't bring a tent or anything as we used an overhanging thorn bush to sleep under.... While we were camping we invited the Youngs to have supper with us. We waited and waited and then went to bed after a quick supper. About 10 minutes afterwards we saw the Youngs' car coming! Hurriedly, Mum and Dad got out of their nighties and pyjamas and into their normal clothes just in time because the Youngs' car arrived that very moment! We had another supper this time (a bigger one). Then we all had a good laugh about what had happened.'[16]

In Zambia sickness can strike suddenly and unexpectedly. In 1990 there was a cholera outbreak in Zambia and all schools including Chengelo were closed for a few weeks. Lusaka with its high water table was particularly badly affected and several hundred children died. The following year Traugott Hartmann, who had been a missionary in Zambia for seventeen years without ever catching malaria, was taken seriously ill with cerebral malaria. The doctors lost hope for him, but people all over the country were praying for him and he made a remarkable recovery. Neil Solomon became ill with hepatitis. He used the opportunity of his enforced idleness to think through a lot of issues. David Rust commented that Neil wrote down his thoughts and gave 'the staff a very strong lead for the start of term – just what was needed to bring everybody in line! I do like working with him – he's got so many ideas, and he's a very positive person. He certainly gives Rachel and I lots of scope to get our ideas established.'[17]

David organised another of his military weekends with a mixture of drill, camouflage, a design competition, the ambushing of staff and night exercises under a full moon. 'I'll never forget the boys who came running to the fire at the base with red ants all over them. The girls there didn't know what to do when the boys frantically stripped off, hopping around the fire like Indians doing a war dance.'[18]

In a letter dated 13th December 1991, David Rust described the term as the best ever. He had taken his children to Ndubaluba and camped under a mango tree. Becky was the cook, Jonny in charge of the fire and Helen looked after the bedding. But sickness was still a recurrent theme. The son of the head of the Australian Baptist Mission had been rushed to hospital with an unknown disease. This was then diagnosed as rabies and the boy died an agonising death. A missionary friend and Gordon Blower of MMM had advanced cancer. An expatriate farmer had just died from AIDS mixed with rabies. The father of one of the schoolboys, who had lost a mother two years ago, had died from AIDS. Two of the domestic staff were dying of AIDS, and within four weeks had grown visibly thinner and more haggard. There had been armed robberies on the Sucklings and Bentleys in Mwinilunga. Bandits from Zaire had fired over their heads as they were forced to lie on the ground. Two vehicles were stolen but by the grace of God both were recovered.

David apologised if parts of his letter came over morbid. 'I suppose it shows that we live quite close to these realities here —and have constantly to rely upon God for his protection and guidance. Answered prayers are a daily reality.'[19]

In Zambia new elections had been held in 1991 and President Kenneth Kaunda and his United National Independence Party (UNIP) were defeated and succeeded by President Frederick Chiluba and his Movement for Multi-Party Democracy (MMD). The Church had prayed long and hard for these elections, which were notable in Africa for the peaceful transfer of power from an incumbent president.

Rachel Rust's health was a continuing anxiety. 'Rachel has to go carefully. Without realising it, like today, she overdoes it and then collapses exhausted and has to spend the next day recovering.'[20] In November of the previous year, Rachel had collapsed and had to be taken to Lusaka lying on a mattress in the back of the school pick-up. Keith and Barbara Rushby went with her, and next day drove her on to Harare. It took several days before word came through that she had been admitted to a private hospital run by nuns. Rachel returned in due course to Chengelo, but her poor health ultimately meant that the Rusts were forced to return to England.

On 2nd April 1990 Terence Musuku of *The Times of Zambia* wrote a full feature on Chengelo School. He was clearly impressed by what he saw: 'In the provision of good secondary education, taking into account – academic, moral, spiritual and physical values – the multi-million Kwacha Chengelo secondary school, set up by Mkushi Farm-block commercial farmers, is probably second to none in Zambia.... As its name denotes light, Chengelo is serving as a torch-light emitting educational light throughout Zambia.' Chengelo was now firmly on the map in Zambia.

## The Formal Opening of Chengelo, 15th May 1993

On 15th May 1993, Brigadier General Godfrey Miyanda, Minister without Portfolio, later Minister of Education, and subsequently Vice-President, came to perform the formal opening of Chengelo School. In addressing the students the Minister said:

*We live in a beautiful country. God has endowed Zambia with abundant natural resources. As we look around us we see something of the beauty of God's creation. Its conservation lies in the hands of you, the young people of Zambia. In many countries, development has resulted in the destruction of natural resources and pollution of the environment. We are determined that this will not happen here and to underline the importance that the MMD Government places on this our President has set up a Ministry of Environment.*

*As you spend these years of your lives at Chengelo set in this lovely part of the country, I hope that you will develop a love for nature that will never leave you.*

*You are privileged indeed to attend a school with the facilities that you see developing around you, and to be taught by staff who are totally dedicated to providing you with the best possible education. But what you must always remember is that with privilege goes responsibility. When you leave this school you will bear a responsibility to those less fortunate than yourselves. A responsibility to use the education that you have received here not only to enrich yourself and improve your position in society but also to serve the community amongst whom you live.*

*This school has been operating for nearly five years now. It is therefore significant that the governing body chose to wait until most of the basic building development was over before the opening of the school. This has given Chengelo the opportunity to prove its worth to all who gather here today.*

*May God bless all who pass through the doors of this institution. Ladies and gentlemen, staff and pupils, I am grateful for the honour of being the one to declare that Chengelo Secondary School is now officially open.*

**Notes**

[1] *Chengelo: The First Three Years*, p. 111.

[2] Mkushi Christian Fellowship Newsletter dated 28th November 1989.

[3] *Chengelo: The First Three Years*, p. 107.

[4] The daily routine according to the Staff Handbook published in October 1999 is as follows:

06.00 Rise. 06.15 Duties. 06.30 Quiet Time. 06.45 Breakfast (three sittings). 07.20 Assembly/Tutor Time (Whole School:

M, W, F; Upper School: Th; Lower School: Tu). 07.45 Lesson 1. 08.30 Lesson 2. 09.15 Lesson 3. 10.00 Break. 10.30 Lesson 4. 11.15 Lesson 5. 12.00 Lesson 6. 12.45 Morning School ends. 12.50 Lunch (three sittings). Rest until 14.05. 14.15 Lesson 7. 15.00 Lesson 8. 15.45 Lessons end. 15.45-17.15 Sports/Free time. 17.40 Duties. 17.55 Supper. 18.40 Prep. (F1+2 in dining hall ends 20.00; F3+4+5 in classrooms ends 20.30). 20.45 Form 1 Lights Out. 21.00 Form 2 Lights Out. 21.15 Form 3 Lights Out. 21.30 Form 4 Lights Out. 21.45 Form 5 Lights Out.

[5] *Chengelo: The First Three Years*, p. 97.

[6] SURE sadly only lasted for a while before the daily programme had to omit it in order to make space for other things.

[7] Op. cit., p. 99.

[8] Ibid., p. 98f.

[9] Ibid., p. 103.

[10] Ibid., p. 102.

[11] Ibid., p. 59.

[12] Undated letter from Rachel Rust to Mum and Dad.

[13] Letter from David to family dated 25th July.

[14] Letter from David to family dated 15th September.

[15] Op. cit., p 62.

[16] Letter from Rebecca Rust to grandparents dated 04.12.90.

[17] Letter from David Rust to parents dated 28.05.91.

[18] Ibid.

[19] Letter from David Rust to his family dated 13.12.91.

[20] Ibid.

# Chapter Five

# The Staff

### Neil Solomon: An Inspirational Leader

All those who knew him speak of Neil Solomon as being an inspirational leader. Barbara Rushby said, 'We held Neil in the very highest regard. He was a lovely man and set a wonderful tone for the school. He had a lovely combination of relaxation and discipline. One day, I remember, he was sitting on a step of the verandah of the farmhouse. He was casually dressed and a lot of pupils were just milling around him. But despite the informality, you knew that he was sitting there totally in charge.' David Moffat said:

*Neil was a remarkable man who had ten good ideas before breakfast. Nine would be impracticable but one would be an absolute winner. He did so many innovative things. He had an amazing relationship with the students. He was the sort of man who could play around with the kids and be absolutely relaxed. On one occasion he asked some kids what they would like to do and one said, I would like to tip a bucket of whitewash over you. So he took his shirt off and with all the children around this chap tipped a bucket of whitewash over the headmaster. If there was a nonsense going on and Neil came into the dining-hall and clicked his fingers he had instant control, for there was not a boy or a girl who did not recognise that Neil was in charge. On one occasion they had a musical disco thing and Neil, who was very wiry, was dressed up as an Indian like Gandhi, and he was doing a dance and all the school was shouting, Go Solly, Go Solly. It never affected his authority. And the kids would say if you do anything wrong, look over your shoulder and Mr Solomon would be there. He knows exactly where you are.*

*Neil had no problems about a little physical chastisement and he would use the cane but not excessively. His policy was that he would never cane a boy unless the boy agreed that he deserved to be caned. One day I met him and he said, 'I feel absolutely awful.' I asked him why and he explained that he had to discipline a certain boy. This boy was a very naughty boy. Neil explained why he was going to spank him and the boy agreed that he deserved it. He bent over and received his five or six strokes. The little boy stood up and came over to Neil with tears in his eyes and put his arms around him and said, 'Th ... Than ... Thank you, Sir.'*

One regular feature of the Solomon era was that new pupils would be introduced to the school by arriving a day before the other pupils. Along with other special activities, Neil Solomon would take the new pupils for a walk up the Chilongoma Hills, or down to the Mkushi river or to the Kingdoms' dam. This provided a wonderful opportunity for the headmaster to get to know each new boy and girl, and for them to get to know him and their fellow pupils.

Neil enjoyed climbing the Chilongoma Hills and seeing the school from that high vantage point. It also provided a marvellous situation for praying over the school. In the August 1990 Prayer and Information Letter, the Headmaster wrote: 'I often climb the Chilongoma hills above the school and look down at the insignificance of the white-washed buildings set amidst the developing lawns, garden and sportsfields, surrounded by the farming lands and the indigenous miombo woodland. It all seems so little and yet how much has been achieved in our two-year history. 100 children are being educated in more than the conventional sense of the word. Through the concerted efforts of eight teachers and seven support staff we are preparing our pupils for a brighter future. We pray that their time at Chengelo will help them find a role which will affect the future of Zambia.'

Neil and Ruby Solomon evolved the practice of getting up at five o'clock every morning, because they found that they could do so much more when they were fresh and undisturbed, and it also made it easier to go to sleep at ten at night when the generator went off. In addition Neil Solomon formed a '15 Club', which met every Monday, Wednesday and Friday morning at 6.00 am to go for a fifteen minute run. As he told his parents it required strict self-discipline to be a member. 'You have to make sure that you go to bed with running and school clothes all ready by the bed, and cupboard tidy and floor swept. Members report to the classroom area at 5.55 for warm-up stretching exercises done in silence. We don't talk until we are out of the built-up area. We then run for 7½ minutes, and then turn. Theoretically everyone should therefore finish at once. They then have 15 minutes to shower and change to be ready for the 6.30–6.45 quiet time that is compulsory in each hostel.... I don't have many members!!! It's easier for a week or so but once the crunch set in membership dropped significantly.'[1]

At 6.30 every morning Neil met with what he called his 'small committee', seven boys and girls from the senior class. They were writing a novel with Neil as editor. It was a crime novel set in Rwanda, which was a pseudonym for Zambia. It all took place around the school, which was being used as a base by the crooks who were involved in a plot to steal copper cathode lorries travelling to Tanzania. The aim of the project was to sell the novel to raise funds for the planned new senior hostels.

## Problems Galore

When the Headmaster gave his report to the Board of Governors on the 16th June 1990, he was entering into his second contract. He wrote: 'Yesterday, two years ago, we arrived in Mkushi overladen with canoe and trailer, expectant and excited. Here we are 24 months later, perhaps a little more jaded, a little wiser, but as excited about the future and more secure in our expectations.' But his report did not make happy reading. There were all sorts of problems both amongst the staff and pupils.

How did Neil Solomon cope with this aggregation of problems? He told the Governors, 'God has given Ruby and me the strength to cope. There is no doubt of that. In recent weeks, people have often remarked on how torn-apart we must feel. Frustrated, irritated, impatient, yes, but never to the point where it weakens us. The last two weeks of last term were emotionally the most difficult two weeks of my life, but we came through stronger than before.' Neil's faith remained undimmed. 'I take up my second contract knowing that we face a future bright with the light of God's blessing.'

But the load resting on a headmaster rarely lessens. In March 1991 Neil Solomon was having to write a personal letter to parents. 'Perhaps you have already heard about this week's disturbances at Chengelo. To dispel rumour and distortion I have decided to write to let you know that two boys were discovered to have visited the girls' hostel after lights out. As a result they and the three girls most involved, have been suspended from the school. Whether they return to Chengelo is a decision which the Board of Governors will take at a specially convened meeting next week.' The Headmaster went on to say that these kinds of incidents are normally kept quiet, but he is having to write to counter rumours which have been spread about Chengelo in the past month. 'I will be frank enough to say that I am disturbed that adults are prepared to accept the often misinformed viewpoint of a child (or the individual behaviour of a small group of children) on which to judge the school. What makes matters worse is that these people are then reporting these rumours as established fact, without consulting me to verify them.'[2] As Neil Solomon told his mother and father, if he had any kind of identity problem, and if he had doubted his calling to Chengelo, he would have been tempted to bale out in the face of these pressures. But his faith held strong.

It was Neil Solomon who was inspirational in the writing of *Chengelo: The First Three Years*, which was edited by his assistant, Anne Carrington. The booklet is a record of the period from September 1988 to December 1991 written by the pupils themselves, the pioneers, and 'dedicated to the Lord for his Vision, his Leading, his Provision, his Enabling, his Grace in all things to get us to December 1991.' As Neil himself wrote as a foreword, 'It is around the camp-fire that the best stories are told, and some of my fondest Chengelo memories are huddling for warmth around the crackling logs, coffee in hand, listening with amusement to tales of pupil nostalgia.'

## Michael Chesterman

The Governors agreed that Neil Solomon should take a furlough for four months from March 1992. In his absence Michael Chesterman was invited to go out in the dual role of acting Headmaster and educational consultant. Michael had had a distinguished career in Zambia. He was teaching at Gresham's School in Norfolk when he made a tentative enquiry about a vacancy for Headmaster at St Mark's, Mapanza, the Anglican secondary school in the Southern Province. He received a three-word telegram from Oliver Green-Wilkinson, the then Archbishop of Central Africa. In peremptory terms the telegram read, 'Come at once.' After his appointment at Mapanza expired, Michael became the Secretary for the Christian Medical Association of Zambia. In this capacity for some six years Michael travelled widely throughout the eight provinces of Zambia. He then accepted the appointment of Headmaster at Mpelembe School, a specialist school run by the Zambian Copper Mining Company, which took sixth-formers in Maths, Physics and Science.

Michael and Sylvia's Bush Telegraph gives a graphic picture of their short time at Chengelo:

*March 1992… I am writing this after dark, by the light of an emergency car battery striplight, rigged up just outside the mosquito net in our bedroom. The generator packed up this morning…. Ah well, supper by candlelight was romantic, the fridge works on paraffin, and the solar-powered torch we brought with us was a good buy.*

*On my desk at the office is a sheet of paper with an outline sketch of the next stage of the building programme. Where are we going to locate the new admin block, staffroom, Headmaster's office, the toilets, computer room, new generator house, staff housing, sports facilities? Where is the money going to come from?*

*…There are of course big problems to overcome. The newspaper headline on the day we flew in was 'Disaster' —referring not to our arrival but the drought. Zambia's maize harvest this year will be nearer 4 or 5 million bags rather than the 12 it should be. The welcome change in the political climate (to multi-party democracy) can't suddenly transform the economy.*

During his six months at Chengelo, Michael had the privilege of having tea with President Frederick Chiluba at State House. Michael interviewed the President as a prospective parent. In due course the President's son, Castro Chiluba, was accepted and entered Chengelo in Form 3.

In the year 2002 Michael Chesterman answered an urgent appeal for an English teacher and returned to Chengelo as a volunteer class teacher for one term. Michael found that in his Form 2 class, he had Chipo Mwanawasa, the daughter of the next President of Zambia.

## Brian Mather

After five years as Headmaster Neil Solomon resigned to take up his research, writing and outdoor interests. Ian Richardson took over for two terms as acting Headmaster[3] until the new man arrived. He was Brian Mather and he started as Headmaster in the third term of 1994. Brian Mather had taught in various schools in England, and had served as an examiner for two examination boards. In 1990 he was appointed to the staff of St John's College in Johannesburg, where he was housemaster to 100 boys as well as having teaching and other responsibilities. Brian was married with three children and was an ordained minister in the International Federation of Christian Churches.

Brian Mather had a wide vision for the development of Chengelo. He envisaged the establishment of a primary school, a sixth form offering Advanced Level in the context of a Christian leadership venture and an outdoor education centre. He hoped to explore the possibility of a Christian teacher training college at Chengelo. He was keen also to face the challenge of the social uplift of the 200 full-time workers, and their families, engaged in building and development projects at the school.

However, Brian Mather announced that he was resigning for personal reasons. He left the school at the end of 1995.

## Ian and Alison Richardson

Ian Richardson, who had been both Deputy Head and Acting Head during his time at Chengelo, was appointed as the new Headmaster with effect from January 1996. In the Newsletter he confessed that things had not been easy during the latter part of 1995, but there was a renewed unity and enthusiasm, which was a real answer to prayer. He wrote: 'I believe that God is fulfilling a promise given in Jeremiah 32:39, "I will give them singleness of heart and action, so that they will always fear me for their own good and the good of their children after them.'"[4] Amongst the changes that Ian Richardson announced were:

- The appointment of Tim Sims and Mike Carter as deputy heads.
- Personal, Social and Moral Education lessons for all pupils, taught from a Zambian Christian perspective.
- Bemba lessons for Forms 1 and 2.
- A completely re-written set of rules, reduced from 14 pages to 1!

'God is really challenging us as a fellowship and staff to commit every area and detail to Him in prayer so that all the glory will go to Him. We believe that God will make Chengelo a place, "...that will bring me renown, joy, praise and honour before all nations on earth that hear of all the good things I do for it" (Jeremiah 33:9).'

Ian and Alison Richardson were challenged about serving in Africa whilst at Spring Harvest, a Christian holiday week in England. Both were then teaching in Bristol, and felt that God was calling them overseas when they got married. They applied to various mission agencies and overseas schools but nothing suitable came up. Then some friends told them about Chengelo. Neil Solomon had preached at the friends' church and said that their most urgent staffing needs were for a secondary Science teacher and a primary teacher. As it happened this exactly matched the Richardsons' qualifications, and a meeting was quickly arranged with Neil. So just under a year later in August 1990, the Richardsons flew out to Zambia.

Alison had never flown before and Zambia was only a place recently discovered on the map. She was frightened of the dark and encountering spiders and snakes. Some fourteen years later, the Richardsons were still at Chengelo, but as we shall learn in Chapter 12 they are being called to move on. Ian is now the school Principal and Alison the Headteacher of the primary school. For their two children, Philippa and Daniel, Chengelo is home. They find it a struggle when they go on leave to the UK, for in Chengelo the children have much more space and freedom to do things. The children have also benefited from having both sets of grandparents visit them more than once, and Alison's parents, Roy and Oriel Fellowes, came out and worked as houseparents for some four years.

## John and Mwaka Ngulube

After Florida Mutambo, John Ngulube is the longest serving Zambian on the teaching staff. John comes from the Eastern Province, and was educated at Katete and at the University of Zambia, where he studied Mathematics. After graduating, John took up a teaching post at the Kenneth Kaunda Secondary School in Chinsali. He first heard about Chengelo from Everist Kabwe, the General Secretary of the Fellowship of Evangelical Students. He applied for a post as a Science and Maths teacher, and was offered a job and joined Chengelo in January 1990. John married Mwaka Chabatama in August 1990, and the couple have a daughter and two sons. In addition, the Ngulubes have taken a niece into their family, as her mother has died. All four children attend the school. As a committed Christian John had enjoyed engaging with students through Scripture Union, which has had a significant work in secondary schools in Zambia since the days of Independence in 1964. In his fourteen years at Chengelo, John has been much involved in discipleship groups, and in student worship activities. It has been his joy to see many young people coming to faith in Christ, and seriously following him after leaving the school.

John Ngulube believes that education is crucial to tackling such problems as poverty and AIDS in Zambia. In the nation generally too many students drop out at Grade 9, instead of going on to school certificate level and then looking for further training. Christians also have a responsibility in nation building. 'The Church should be active in education not just passive. The Church must stand up and teach what is right. Corruption is a problem in every society. But I believe that you cannot beat corruption if the heart is not changed in the first place. We are corrupt people. We can do things to mitigate corruption but look at the pay that policemen get. It is very, very little.... Temptations are real. The little money that people get is not enough to sustain them to the end of the month.... I will always be optimistic about the future. I believe that there are people in this country who should rise up and try and help society in whatever way. I am always going to be optimistic about this nation because the potential is there.'[5]

## Roger and Angie Allen

Roger and Angie Allen came back from honeymoon in 1991 and found a letter waiting them from David Rust. Knowing that they had a heart for Africa, David suggested that teaching at Chengelo would be right up their street. So a meeting was arranged with Neil Solomon, who was passing through Bristol, where Roger and Angie were teaching at Oakhill School run by the Bristol Christian Fellowship. A year later the Allens found themselves at Chengelo. Whilst Angie looked after the staff primary school children, Roger became Head of Humanities and took over teaching History from David Rust. Also together with Roy Fellowes he set up Religious Studies as a class subject.

Angie, once she had got over her fear of snakes and spiders, was determined that she was going to listen and learn. 'The biggest challenge for me was having somebody working in the house with me – for we all had housemaids – trying to work with somebody who didn't speak any English.'[6] She discovered that the food was generally a very Western diet. There were no great shortages but it could be limited. 'We got pretty sick and tired of cabbage and pumpkin and rice with stones in it.' There was a period when they had nothing but ravioli when a huge consignment of ravioli tins was donated to the school.

Chocolate became the ultimate luxury.

The Allens lived in the old farmhouse, and Roger had only to walk 42 steps to the History classroom. It was quite a contrast to commuting in the Bristol traffic. They arrived at the end of a drought when it had not rained for eight or nine months. The first time it rained there was dancing outside the classroom. The rain came and it disappeared like a sponge. There was only one phone on the site, that in the headmaster's office. Angie rang her mother in England in great excitement. 'It's raining here. It's raining here.' And her mother said, 'Oh, it's been raining here for the past three weeks!'

All the water in the house came down from the furrow on the Moffats' farm. When they ran a bath, they would sometimes find a tadpole or other objects in the water. One day the Rushbys found that their pipe was firmly blocked by a fish. Angie said, 'The water was really brown, and when I got in I wondered whether I was going to be any cleaner when I get out of this bath.' They only had the generator for power, which came on at 07.30 and went off at 12.30 or 13.00, and then came on again at 17.30 and went off bang on 22.00. So candles were a necessity, but people tended to go to bed early because everything started early in the morning. If there was thunder or lightning around, all electrical equipment and computers had to be unplugged, or else there was a danger of losing everything.

On one occasion the staff put on a play, *The Happiest Days of our Life*. It was all very British. Roger played the Vicar and Angie his wife. Ian Richardson had the main role in which he fell in love with the character played by Ruby Solomon. At the dress rehearsal, Ian did not know any of his lines. But he read them through that night, and when it came to the real thing he knew the whole part word for word.

A crisis came to Chengelo when the boiler exploded in the boys' hostel. There was a faulty valve, which stuck so that the pressure built up in the old 44-gallon drum of hot water. Neil Solomon was talking to somebody, and narrowly missed being hit by a concrete block which landed nearby. Another block embedded itself in one of the classroom walls. Mercifully nobody was sitting in the boys' toilet since the pipe shot right across where the legs would have been. When pressure release valves were later fitted, a whistling sound would indicate overheating, and then it would be a matter of rushing around to turn on all the taps to reduce the pressure.

Like many English expatriates the Allens came out somewhat starry-eyed. They grieved to see the conditions for some of the workers. But over time they saw very real improvements in those conditions, such as the provision of low cost houses made with concrete blocks. Initially some of the staff put electricity into the workers' homes, but this was a bit of a Heath Robinson venture. On one occasion when there was a lightning storm, and the whole atmosphere was electric, somebody was running around the compound screaming because the electricity had not been properly earthed. Now there is mains electricity as well as decent tap water and a well-equipped clinic in the compound.

After two years at Chengelo, Roger took a sabbatical to do a course in Development Studies at Norwich. On his return Roger, together with Tim Sims, started Development Studies as a curriculum subject, which meant that he was dealing with many issues highly relevant to Zambia, such as foreign debt and sustainable development. The Allens finally left Chengelo in 1999. For them it had been a time of much learning and personal growth. They took back to England wonderful memories of camping trips and sitting around open fires with pupils or staff friends. For Roger, 'The number one memory is the African moon. We used to walk under a full moon where the stars are so much closer because there are no streetlights to block them. And we would be pushing a pram with our three month-old baby, and our little cat running along behind us with its tail up in the air.'

Friendships were formed right across the white and black barriers. Roger is still in touch with two sets of brothers, Daniel and Samuel Pedersen and their best friends, Lombe and Wembe Malama. 'Actually all are very committed Christians and much involved in their local churches.' Now back in the UK, Roger is using his knowledge of Zambia and Development Studies in his work with Christian Aid. His big regret about living in England is that his children cannot go to Chengelo, 'the best school I have ever known.'

## Mark and Ros Newhouse

Mark and Ros Newhouse and their two daughters, Sarah, aged six, and Alicia, aged four, arrived from Perth, Australia in January, 1992. Mark came to teach Maths and Ros to help as a science lab technician. It was a shock for them to encounter the badly potholed road, the frequent roadblocks with soldiers armed with AK47s, and the beggars in the towns. Mark got sick with a tummy bug, diarrhoea and a headache ('Mkushi Belly'), and Ros had frequent bursts of weeping, feeling homesick, stressed, worried and fearful. But they soon settled, and as they neared the end of their two-year contract, Mark was asked to stay on as acting Deputy Head. Interestingly enough, although Mark initially said, 'no', it was Ros who was keen that they should pray about it, and in due course they agreed to the request.

In addition to the teaching, Mark got involved with expeditions to Kundalila Falls, Kasanka Game Park and Mount Mpumpu. In his innocence he had imagined that life in Zambia would be considerably less busy than back in Australia. He soon learnt that this was an idle fantasy. Mark's diary for the 11th January 1993 read:[7]

*Getting prepared for the new term has been an exhausting time. I had to move the Maths classroom to a new room;*

*prepare the sports program; we welcomed Les and Bronwyn Mutton from Western Australia and helped them settle in; I set up the Kafue hostel for Peter and Jane Guest and did the initial houseparenting; I ran two houseparents meetings, a Maths Department meeting, attended EXCO, Heads of Department and two general staff meetings. I was then on duty for the first Monday, again inducting a new staff member.*

In July 1992 Mark was invited by Neil Solomon to be a member of the school Executive Committee. Mark's diary entry for the 16th October 1993 read:

*Being on the Executive Committee has given me a close view of the development and direction of the school. Increasingly Exco has taken over the initiative on decision making from the Board. We make all the decisions on staffing, fees, vehicle purchasing, salaries, workers' conditions, school programme etc. I think the most significant development in the past two years has been the progress of professionalism. ...Exco meets fortnightly, usually for about 2½ hours.*

At the end of his time in Chengelo in October 1994, Mark wrote: 'I've enjoyed living here so much that it doesn't excite me to think of suburban life, driving to work each day and paying off the bills and the mortgage.' His words could be echoed by the great majority of expatriate teachers on leaving the school.

### Mike and Val Hackston

Val and Mike Hackston served at Chengelo for five years from the beginning of 1993 to the end of 1997. Val was Brian Mathers' and then Ian Richardson's secretary and Mike looked after the Science Department. He ran the Christian choir and took an active role in the Sunday celebrations. They describe their time in Chengelo as 'immensely fulfilling and challenging'. The first challenge was coping 'with the pressures that a boarding school presents when your home is a matter of metres away from a hostel full of teenagers. ...A second challenge was the need to work with other Christians whose views on how things should be done was different from one's own.'[8] Mike Hackston is now a Trustee of the Chengelo Educational Trust in the UK and acts as membership secretary.

## Tim and Denise Sims

Tim Sims is a man small in stature but big in character. He and Denise were to play significant roles in the development of Chengelo during their eleven years at the school. They arrived in February 1993 with their two daughters, Hannah and Emily. Tim was a Geography teacher, but during his time at Chengelo found himself teaching most subjects. Denise taught Biology and Geography. In due course Tim was appointed Head of Sixth Form in January 2000, and subsequently Head of the secondary school in May 2002. He knew how to delegate and to hold others accountable for their areas of responsibility. By concentrating on the educational side, he played a key role in the raising of standards all round.

Tim is also a first class preacher and used his keen analytical mind to open up and apply the Biblical text with great skill and poignancy. His musical skill and sensitivity were great gifts in leading worship in Mkushi Christian Community. He was a much-valued elder of the North Church. Denise had a real heart to minister to others of all races and backgrounds. She was a woman of prayer, and her compassion and sensitivity meant that she was able to give much support to many of the women at Chengelo, as well as many pupils and their families. When the Sims finally returned to the UK, in December 2004, their wise and spiritual leadership was much missed.

## Senior Management Team

Having been Headteacher of the secondary school for some six years, Ian Richardson was appointed Principal of the school in 2002. Before that there had been two

Headteachers (one for the secondary, and one for the primary) of equal status, who shared overall responsibility for the oversight of the Site Manager, the Office Manager, the Farm Manager, and the Manager of the Ndubaluba outdoor centre. This was an unwieldy structure, so it was decided to appoint a Principal who would co-ordinate the work of the managers, the two school heads and their deputies. Thus was born the Senior Management Team. Tim Sims became responsible for the secondary school and Alison took over the primary school. In addition the Principal looks after the recruitment of staff, publicity and the pastoral care of the staff. The Principal also has an input in any serious disciplinary matter. The aim is to ensure the unity of Chengelo with a single Christian ethos. Looking back over fourteen years, Ian Richardson has seen the school grow from a small campus with some 100 pupils and 12 staff to the present extensive campus with some 400 pupils and 80 staff.

**Salaries and Work Permits**
Chengelo's policy on staff salaries is to pay a reasonable living wage. But in addition the school provides free housing, medical cover, electricity, water, and a maid service, as well as free lunches for staff, and free schooling for up to three children. However the low pay can make it difficult to recruit both local and expatriate staff, who can get much better salaries in other independent schools in Zambia, as well as in some neighbouring countries and overseas. Martin Solomon, the Zambian Office Manager, was employed on expatriate terms in Botswana, and took a substantial cut in salary to move back to Zambia, because he felt that God was calling him to work in Chengelo.

So far as expatriate teachers are concerned, one of the big headaches for Chengelo is getting work permits. Many hours are spent in correspondence, on the phone and in visits to the Immigration Department to get the necessary authorisation for desperately-needed staff members.

## Zambian Staff

Apart from having the right qualifications, and if possible previous teaching experience, the Governors have taken the view that staff recruited for Chengelo should have a clear understanding of Christian education, and share the vision of Chengelo as a Christian school. In addition it is felt that applicants should have known a definite call from God to serve in the school. A difficulty in recruiting Zambian nationals for staff appointments is not merely finding those who meet these requirements, but competing with the enormous demand and opportunities for Christian teachers both in Zambia and elsewhere. Furthermore it has to be faced that the rural situation of Chengelo is a definite drawback.

The teaching staff has gone from a situation where Zambians were a distinct minority to one where over half are Zambian, and all the administrative staff are Zambian. The Senior Management Team was all expatriate apart from Martin Solomon, but from 2005 has been strengthened by the appointment of Jani Zabangwa as Head of Staff Development. Martin as Office Manager handles a budget of $1.5 m, so he has great responsibility. Both the Principal and Governors recognise the need to find high quality Zambians to fill posts in Senior Management. One of the ways that Chengelo has sought to tackle the situation is to encourage existing staff to take additional master's degree courses. At present some six staff are doing this, five of whom are Zambians. Ian Richardson himself did a master's degree at Bath University by correspondence. John Ngulube has also been studying for a master's degree with Bath in educational management. At the time of writing, he is awaiting the marking of his dissertation. Others have used the MBA course at Leicester University in educational management.

Part of the school's vision has been to train teachers at Chengelo to the school's own high standards. In Term 2 of 2001, Chengelo had two student PE teachers, Agatha

Phiri and Mercy Kolomwe, from Kwame Nkrumah College, Kabwe. Two men came to Chengelo who were doing their final term training as Maths and French teachers. Priscilla Mwanza successfully completed one year of further teacher training at Chengelo following her B Ed and was taken on as a full time member of staff. One man, who was recruited to work under Steve Bannister, is now the chief sports officer at the University of Zambia.

**Labour Relations**
A vexed issue, which has occupied the management and governors in 2003/04, has been the matter of labour relations. There have been several strikes including one of four days. The policy of the school from the outset was that it would only employ local labour and use local materials, so minimising the amount of money that would be sent out of the region and the country. So Chengelo trained its own carpenters, bricklayers, plumbers, mechanics and other trades so that they could run their own workshops on site. David Moffat, who has been involved in negotiations with the labour force, says, 'Certainly within the Mkushi district Chengelo is the best employer by far. They pay above the average on wages, they provide medical facilities and sports facilities. They do more than anybody else …already things are better.'[9]

**Staff Loyalty**
These incidents should not detract from the loyalty and faithfulness of many of the workers employed at Chengelo. One such couple is Silva and Phyllis Kazhinga. The Kazhingas come from the Ikelenge District of North Western Province. After leaving school, Silva worked for Paul Fisher at Hillwood Farm. In 1986 Silva went to Sachibondu to train under Gordon Suckling in church leadership. In 1990 Silva was sent to Chengelo to work for a few months in order to earn money to buy his own tools, and 13 years later he was still working there. He

was employed as foreman of the carpentry shop with fourteen men working under him. But in addition he was an elder at the church that meets at David Moffat's farm. During Pastor Joe Chikoti's lifetime they saw the church built up to a congregation averaging 120 persons on a Sunday. Phyllis was active in the church, heading the work amongst the women.[10]

Barton Young, one of the founding fathers, speaks with pride of the quality of the staff, both expatriate and Zambian. He singled out amongst many Zambians, John Ngulube for his commitment and ability to minister to his own people; Saul Tembo, the Art and Design teacher, who is also a great man of God, able to minister to educated Zambians, and currently doing a study course in Christian ministry; Martin Solomon, who took over as Office Manager from Brian Bentley, and whose wife, Kukeña, is an extremely able teacher of Geography; and Chris Banda, the Librarian, Pastoral Head and Houseparent of the Junior Boys' Hostel, a man wholly committed to the vision of Chengelo.

John Ngulube benefited greatly from an exchange set up for him by David Rust with his comprehensive school, Katharine Lady Berkeley School in Wootton-under-Edge, Gloucestershire. John was there for two months and he was followed in due course by Kukeña Solomon (a three week stay) and Saul Tembo (five weeks). Saul Tembo was the artist in residence and with the aid of over 250 pupils created a large African mural in the centre of the school, which attracted a great deal of interest from the local community and press. All were wonderful ambassadors for Zambia and for Christ. In 2002 three teachers, Robin Warren, Chris Penna and David Rust, himself, from Katharine Lady Berkeley School came on a ten-day exchange visit to Chengelo. There are many other teachers, local and expatriate, who have played, or are still playing, a vital role in the development of the Chengelo vision. These teachers are mentioned in Appendix 1.

Russell Wyatt, looking back over sixteen years, is enormously impressed by the quality of the staff. He can only see the hand of God in the process of appointments. His sister who has been involved in staff selection elsewhere told Russell, 'I don't know how you do it. We have a pedantic system of selection but we still seem to get misfits. You don't have much of a system and yet you seem to get some jolly good people.'

**Notes**
[1] Letter dated 05.06.90 from Neil Solomon to his parents Dr and Mrs RA Solomon in Underberg, South Africa.
[2] Letter to parents dated 14.03.91.
[3] It is interesting to note that in a meeting with the founding fathers dated 30th October 1993, Dr Alan Staples of Treverton College had actually recommended that Ian Richardson should be confirmed as Headmaster after six months trial as Acting Head.
[4] *Chengelo Educational Trust Newsletter*, February 1996, No. 4.
[5] Author's interview with John Ngulube, 20.05.04.
[6] Quotations from author's interview with Roger and Angie Allen, 19.03.04.
[7] Email to author dated 14.06.05.
[8] *Chengelo Educational Trust Newsletter*, December 2000, No. 13.
[9] Interview with author 16.05.04.
[10] *Chengelo Educational Trust Newsletter*, No. 19, 2003.

# Chapter Six

# The Pupils

**Witnesses to the Light**

At the end of the first term in 1988, the Headmaster sent out a newsletter to all parents. Neil Solomon wrote, 'We are very much aware that without the children, this school would be a mere collection of buildings' but that it was with a 'feeling of awe and gratitude to God that we contemplate 12 weeks that have far exceeded our expectations. Starting a new school has its problems: Rules must be tested and tried, discarded or reinforced, traditions are established, facilities are all in the process of development. But there are also the joys of a new creation —a freshness and vigour that are unsullied by old habits. Staff and pupils alike have enjoyed the pioneering spirit, as with prayer and reflection, through trials, success and failure we forge a mould for Chengelo. Here I must pay tribute to the pupils. Although they must sometimes get the impression that they are a source of great worry to the teachers, they have overall been a collective inspiration in their response to a new situation. It is our sincere belief that they will indeed be a "witness to the light" in the future years of Zambia.'

## My Hiding Place

The pioneers responded enthusiastically to the new school. For some they found life at school even more interesting than life at home. One parent wrote to the school, 'The last half-term my son complained that he was bored (at home) as the school has so much more to offer over the weekends.' For some of the children, Chengelo was not only a fine school, but it also offered a place of safety and escape from the harsh world outside. In a remarkable essay, which was included in *Chengelo: The First Three Years*, Esther Kamata wrote about her hiding place up in a tree, which, whilst not specifically relating to Chengelo, could have applied to the school. [1]

*In this world of bribery and corruption, hatred and betrayal, dishonesty, poverty and sadness, I never dreamed there could be a place as beautiful as this. From one extreme to another, I find myself here, dumbfounded and perplexed. From the screaming of the baby, the yelling of the father and the nagging of the mother, I find myself here. Like a miracle I am saved; saved from the outside world; stepping up, away from everyone and everything that brings grief....*

*My new world invites me into a feeling of warmth and security. I gladly step in, fed up with the insecurity of the old world. I am above the rest; not in superiority, but above the feelings of this world. Look up! The heavens are so near, close enough for me to reach out and touch if I stretched, I am sure. I am close now, I need not worry. The thought of all the criticism and condemnation draws me closer [to] the one and only one who never criticises or condemns me. I feel free, secure and important. So high up.*

*Hang on... is this world really mine? Will I be able to stay here forever? There I knew nothing could be so perfect. The faint gonging of the village church bell rings out. Why? Why does it have to ruin my world? Half an hour more and the father will be home. Then the nagging, then the yelling, then the screaming. Like another miracle, my world changes.... My new world, a fantasy, slowly drifts away as my feet carry me away, back to the bribery and corruption, hatred and betrayal, dishonesty, poverty and sadness. I am stepping once again, but this time, I am stepping down.*

## I Stand Alone?

One of the great truths inculcated at Chengelo is that a man or a woman does not have to be alone to face the realities of a hostile world. A Christian is one who has found a friend and a companion for the journey through life. Anthony Lawrence captured this truth in his work entitled *I Stand Alone.*[2]

*As I stand alone in the middle of this desolate, barren place, I take time to absorb my surroundings.*

*The sun is almost directly above me. I feel as if its rays are focussed on me, and me alone; relentlessly beating down on my helpless body. I have no shelter from my tormentor, nowhere to seek refuge from the blazing heat. Strangely a cool breeze blows along the forest plain, offering me a mild form of cooling comfort. My consolation is short lived. The breeze dies away, leaving only the hot, dusty desert air which dries my mouth and gnaws at my lungs.*

*I stand alone as a solitary blade of grass, barely managing to stand upright even in the gentle breeze. I am drained of all life. I need food and water just to be able to stand. The landscape around is continually changing. I have no direction in which to head, and no power to get there. Alone I am nothing. I am a self-supporting being who needs support.*

*I stand alone. The silence is deafening and terrifying. I may plead for help as loudly as I can, but there is no one to hear my cries. I am trapped in a wide open space; imprisoned in a cage without bars. I cry out again; there is no reply except the gentle blow of the breeze, I am trapped in another dimension by my deepest but present fear; being lost alone. The monochromatic landscape in which I stand offers no comfort. It is changing, but always remaining the same.*

*I stand alone. I feel like a blemish on this desert surface, that will eventually be removed. I now have no fear of being alone, as I know I have been alone my whole life; my surroundings have only be comforting and consoling me. Now I realise the frailty of man, whether alone in a large city or alone on a desert plain. Without guidance and protection he is nothing. Without God he stands alone.*

## Prefects

It was not until the school had been going for over two years that Chengelo introduced its first prefects. They were Bupe Pihlblad, Gabriel Chansa, Mpande Simumba, Lynette Pollen, Daniela Schempp, Vangela Dakis and Prabjot Matharu. This is how Leah Stephenson described the situation:[3]

*During the first and second years of Chengelo, prefects were not even thought of. Our headmaster did not agree with the idea of prefects at that stage. He trusted us and thought we were all dependable and capable of being responsible for ourselves. All trusted, he let the school run for two and a half years without any appointed head pupils to watch over us.*

*The school increased with another 50 pupils in 1991. Things were not running too smoothly. Pupils started slackening in their work and had too much freedom of time and speech. It was plain disobedience and too many advantages had been taken.*

*Mr Solomon soon introduced prefects. They are appointed to take responsibility in different areas of the school like in the hostels, at meals, prep, detention and Saturday night video when a teacher is not present. They can be consulted if pupils need advice on academic or personal problems.*

*Because of their tiresome duties, prefects are awarded special privileges: a separate dorm in the hostel with a door for privacy; videos on Wednesday nights; they can stay up until 22.00 hours and are given prefects' dinners with the Headmaster. They are trusted by the staff and have the support of staff and pupils. In turn they are responsible for maintaining discipline and the smooth running of the school.*

Michael Chesterman found that he could use the prefects to motivate others into action. The rough couch grass in front of the dining hall needed weeding. 'If I go down on my hands and knees on the grass near the entrance to the dining hall at break time,' said Michael to the prefects, 'will you step forward and join me by weeding by hand? If everyone sees the Headmaster and the prefects giving a lead, how can they refuse to join in?' Risky but it worked.[4]

Now that Chengelo has progressed to having its own sixth form, consideration is once again being given to whether or not to re-introduce prefects, who had been done away with some years ago. The issues are whether to have selected or elected prefects, and how to incorporate the sixth form into a prefect system.

### Chengelo's First Ambassador

In 1991 Mpande Simumba was sent abroad as Chengelo's first ambassador. He went to be an exchange pupil with King's School, Southampton, which is run by the Community Church, Southampton. Mpande was met at Heathrow by Sian and David Fenton-Jones, who had been at Chengelo as volunteers, and then travelled down by train to Southampton to stay with Gwynneth and John Symons, who had pastored Kitwe Chapel for ten years. Mpande said, 'The first day at school was quite nerve-wracking because I didn't know what to expect, and I knew that everybody's eyes were focussed on me.... Thankfully the staff and pupils were friendly and kind and I was made to feel welcome. Their expectations of me were very amusing. Some of them expected me to be a thin young boy, dressed in animal skins and who couldn't speak or understand English.'[5] During his time in England Mpande went on a school trip to the Gower Peninsula in Wales. He spent time working in a solicitor's office and a barrister's chambers. He also managed to get himself thoroughly lost in London when he went to a cinema and missed the last train and bus back to where he was staying. 'In the end we managed to get home at about 2.30, tired, wet and miserable.' Mpande Simumba is now married and living in Manchester, where he runs his own business.

## Planting the Sports Field

One of the most memorable occasions for pupils in the early days of the school was the planting of the sports field. This is how Amy Cantlay remembers this event:[6]

*Drop! Bend! Cover! Stamp! They continued with the same motion again and again occasionally straightening their aching backs to collect another bundle of sodden grass. Every now and again, one glances at his watch and frowns. Why does time pass so slowly when you want it to go fast?*

*When Mr Solomon announced that the whole school would meet at the sports field to plant grass at 15.00 hours, the looks on the faces of the Chengelo pupils said it all! They hated the idea. The groans and grunts of disapproval expressed their disgust at having to do a dirty, sweaty job like that.*

*But, despite all the complaints, everyone arrived promptly at 14.55 (obeying the rule that you have to report to an activity five minutes before it starts) and waited, hoping that something would happen to postpone the tedious job ahead. But as usual, things didn't go their way, and they were each given a line to plant. Work began.*

*The ground was muddy, and murky puddles of water lay everywhere. They made their way slowly down the lines and their feet grew heavier and heavier as the brown, sticky mud collected and refused to be shaken off.*

*As the first people began to finish, a sense of restlessness descended on them; before they knew it, the first mudball flew, then the second, third and fourth until people began to lose count. All those within throwing distance joined in and mud was flying everywhere. What had promised to be*

*a boring, dull job, had turned out to be a lot of fun. I can
assure you that the clothes worn by the pupils that day have
never been the same colour since!*

*Now, a year later, we look at the grass and remember that
grass planting as if it were yesterday. The grass, which has
now started to look strong and healthy, as the rains come
again, has been rolled and sprayed with weed killer. The
broadleaf weed has practically disappeared and so have
the days of planting grass. However the days of those 'good
old days' will always remain and when we see the beautiful
sports field in the future, we will have the satisfaction of
saying, 'we did that....'*

Using the pupils to plant the grass was not only an
exercise to get the job done cheaply and quickly, but it
was a way of bringing home to the pupils that they must
take responsibility for their environment. It also helped
to teach them that there was dignity in manual labour.
This lesson was taught in countless little ways. The pupils
were responsible for cleaning their own classrooms on a
roster basis. They were encouraged to take the initiative
in doing odd jobs that needed doing around the school.
Bupe Pihlblad and Anthony Lawrence took care of the
roundabout in front of the dining-hall. This was a dry area
with a few shrivelled plants. It required a lot of water for
Bupe and Anthony to create two flowerbeds, bordered
with natural white stones, around the base of the trees.
During Term 2 in 1989, pupils were asked to help water
the trees which had been planted in the main entrance
driveway to the school. It was expected that each pupil
would water three trees each. This meant carrying a lot
of buckets of water from the furrow. One pupil, no doubt
following the example of the Prince of Wales, tried talking
and playing his tape recorder to the trees!

## Chengelo Fashions

Chengelo students were not immune to the pressures of a consumerist society. Samuel Pedersen described some of the fashions, which appealed to boys and girls in the early '90s.[7] Shoes had to be those of the right brand. Hair styles, especially one which looked as if an iron was being worn on the head, spread all the way from the United States to Zambia. Some boys in Term 3, 1991, appeared with a trade symbol grooved in their hair on top of the head. This did not impress the staff, who introduced new rules for hairstyles. Boys had to wear short hair and girls had to have long hair tied up. Other fashions which appealed to the young people were: baggy, stone-washed jeans, long baggy bermuda shorts, and skin-tight cycle pants, preferably black with luminous patches or stripes on them. Again the school authorities responded with new school rules. Parents were no doubt grateful that this expensive form of peer competition was outlawed. Parents were constantly reminded about the appropriate length of girls' skirts (knee length), since these showed a steady tendency to creep higher and higher up the thigh. It also became necessary to warn parents that inappropriate music tapes and cassettes would be confiscated.

## The Cantlay and Bentley Families

A number of families have seen all their children go through the school. They have included the Cantlays from the Mkushi Farming Block, and the Bentley family. Dr Amy Kingdom (née Cantlay), who is now the acting district veterinary surgeon in Mkushi, runs the Chengelo Association and has been in touch with over 200 ex-pupils. The *Old Chengelian Newsletter* that came out in 1995 showed former pupils dispersed around the world with numbers in Britain, the United States, and South Africa, as well as in Zambia. Brian and Anne Bentley came to Chengelo in the early '90s. Brian was Administrator until the end of 1998, and then returned as Site Manager for a period. All the four Bentley children went through Chengelo. Brian now runs Action Auto in Kitwe, and a son, Michael, works for Action Auto in Lusaka. Michael married Rachel Overton, one of the primary school teachers, in April 1997. His brother, Garry, also works for Action Auto and is a computor expert. A sister, Sherry, is married to Alex Lilley and runs a silver jewellery business. Patrick, the third brother, is currently at Bath University.

## The Mutala Family

Mpundu Mutala is one of the founding governors of Chengelo School. Mpundu studied in England at All Nations Christian College in Ware, Hertfordshire, and subsequently at Fuller Theological Seminary in Pasadena, California, USA. After working with Scripture Union, he has now been General Secretary of the Bible Society in Zambia for many years. His wife, Leah, heads up the women's work with the Evangelical Fellowship of Zambia. Leah, together with a noble band of women volunteers, brings financial and spiritual help to thousands of orphans, who have lost parents and relatives in the pandemic of HIV/AIDS, which has reduced life expectancy in Zambia to some 42 years. For example, in the township of Matero, outside of Lusaka, there are some five or six thousand orphans, including child-headed families, where a young girl still at school, can find herself responsible for bringing up some five or six siblings.

Mpundu and Leah Mutala are precisely the kind of key workers, for whom Chengelo School was set up to bring help with their children's education. It is therefore wholly appropriate that all five of the Mutala children have passed through Chengelo. The two oldest, Wankunda and Mukontelo Mutala, are currently working and studying in the United States. The two youngest, Ntiusya and Jeremiah, are both still students at Chengelo. Ntiusya is to be the new head girl in 2005.

David Mutala, the third child, is hoping to do his

university studies in America. He was at Chengelo from January 1997 to December 2001. In his final IGCSE, David got four A*s, four As and one B. He has very good memories of his time in the school. He thought Chengelo a very good school, and was impressed with the quality of living in the hostels, the good food, and the excellent standard of teaching. He enjoyed the interaction with his contemporaries, and considered that the 'openness and the sharing of experiences and the helping one another through school was a very enriching experience.'[8] David's favourite subjects were History, Geography and Religious Studies. His worst subject was Maths. He did cross-country running and a lot of outdoor activities. From Forms 3 to 5, David was in the Christian leadership team, which gave a lead at the Sunday evening celebrations, now called Fusion, as well as meeting regularly for Bible study and prayer. If there was a downside to Chengelo, he suggested that it was that the pupils were quite protected and cocooned from the real world.

David believed that Chengelo had inculcated him with values for life centred around the Christian faith, and that this would be something that was going to live with him. He had learnt the importance of good inter-personal relationships, physical well-being, regular exercise, the appreciation of nature, and of being a good citizen. He had been challenged in his Development Studies with Mr Roger Allen to think about what he wanted to do with his life, and what he could do for his country. 'I feel strongly that I would ultimately like to come back and work in my own country. Much as I would like to succeed on the international scene, I think that I would be most fulfilled succeeding right here at home and doing something meaningful for my own people. [This would probably be] working in the private sector and doing things to improve the welfare of ordinary people living in Zambia. Probably that could be achieved using the avenue of business, offering services that help people enjoy a greater dimension of freedom and enrichment in the way that they go about their lives.'[9]

## The Class of '96

The Class of '96, who were in Mrs Smiles' and Mr Van der Maas' form classes, now have their own excellent website,[10] which was set up in New Zealand by Rachel Grindlay. Some of the memories recorded on the website are of climbing up to the Cross on the Chilongoma Hills at Easter, of going on Saturday morning school runs ranging in length from 3km to 10km, of Saturday night videos, of weeding lantana, and of camping on the Heroes and Unity Weekend. The students dug their own toilet areas, built shelters out of old branches, slept directly on the ground, and obeying Mr Solomon's instructions, left no trace of the camp next morning. Singing round the bonfire under the African sky was an unforgettable experience.

Rachel Grindlay also remembers the responsibility ratings, with its system of debits and credits, with each student being assigned a rating from A to H, with A being the highest. A 'C' rating was allowed to bring a radio/cassette player to school, whilst an 'A' rating was pretty free to do anything they wished because they had the trust of the staff. 'I liked the system, though that may be because I was a huge goody-goody and managed to get an "A" rating by the middle of 3rd Form. The ratings system was effective but generally disliked and so was removed around 1995.'[11]

The website for Class of '96 goes on to say the school food that the students just loved to hate included French toast, which could be smelt as one walked over the furrow. This was not normal French toast but bread soaked in oil. 'I'm sure that if you picked it up and squeezed it you could get a cup of oil. Yuck.'[12] Breakfast toast, cooked on the stove, had a strange taste of kerosene. Tea came with milk and two cups of sugar added. Lunch consisted of rice, stew, cabbage (without fail), possibly a sponge cake, but always custard regardless of what the rest of the dessert was. Sunday night dinner was nshima and some kind of relish and everyone's weekly anti-malarial tablet. 'I recall that often half the dining-hall would stand up after grace had been said and walk out. It wouldn't have been so bad if the relishes had been decent. I remember one night we were given bones – I would have felt bad giving my dog something with that little meat on it....' Rachel's happiest times were spent on 'Sunday afternoons relaxing by the pool, with music, friends, and possibly some treasured "tuck"' (food from home). [13]

## Pupil Behaviour

The Waddells recount an incident when their son had a minor brush with authority. A mixed group of friends, including their son, asked for permission to go for 'a walk' to the Mkushi River one Sunday afternoon. Permission was granted provided that they did not go swimming. It was a very hot day and on arrival the water proved too tempting and they succumbed. However the Headmaster was suspicious about this request and went to check up on them. He found some of them in the water and others hiding in the bushes. All the miscreants were ordered back to school and marched into the Headmaster's office.

Whilst the boys were being lectured on their misbehaviour, they found themselves distracted by the sight of Nellie Prentice (whose husband Rob taught art) performing all sorts of acrobatics in her garden in a vain attempt to lure one of her pedigree Siamese cats down from a tree. The boys could not keep a straight face and their sniggers only compounded their offence. The punishment was to lug a number of building blocks by hand from the brick works to the site of the new clinic. It was a considerable distance and the task had to be completed within a time limit. This type of manual labour was a favourite form of punishment at the time of building construction. One pupil distinguished himself by the number of bricks he carried. As an irreverent wag put it, 'Chengelo was built by faith... and Billy Miller.'[14]

In August 1996 the school adopted a discipline policy, which aimed to be redemptive, restoring the pupil to right relationships and behaviour. The model suggested followed that of the coach. 'Now our children are in the game of life for themselves. We can send plays (sic) in from the sidelines and huddle during the time-outs, but we can no longer stop the game and show them how it is done. They are now calling the plays themselves and moving forward.'[15] The sanctions range from warnings, to detentions, to gating and manual labour, and ultimately suspension. The Governors have clearly stated that they want a school, 'where love and understanding replace the need of the cane and replace indifference.' Corporal punishment, which could only be administered by the Head with the consent of two members of staff when all other sanctions had failed, is now no longer used as it is now illegal in Zambia. Chengelo is a Zambian Christian school, which has to operate in a society where promiscuity and AIDS are rife. 'As a result, Zambian Christians have very strong views on boy/girl relationships and even courting couples would never be alone together in a house in order to avoid any hint of sin. For this reason our rules on physical contact are very conservative and strictly enforced.'[16]

**Medical Care**

For a school in the bush of Central Africa with some 400 pupils and a staff of 80 or so, plus their families, medical and nursing care is a vital and necessary ingredient. Sickness and disease can strike suddenly and with little warning.

*April 1992. ...It's all happening! We had just got into our stride when sickness struck. As more and more of the students went down with sickness and vomiting, followed by some of the staff, we realised that this was not just a few*

115

*cases of malaria, but something more serious. First we sent
28 of the boarders home, while we carried on as best as we
could with depleted staff. The telltale sign of yellow faces,
and a visit from the school doctor, confirmed that we were
up against an outbreak of Hepatitis A. So I had to close
the school. This meant sending 200 boys and girls home
without notice (telephones don't work out here in the bush),
arranging buses to come from Lusaka and the Copperbelt
etc. Everyone rallied round, to cope with the situation in a
calm and controlled manner. Now the school is empty. We
are working to trace the source of the bug, and to take
remedial action....* [17]

In addition to the occasional medical crisis there is a
need for regular, routine examinations. 'Dr Andy Patching
is a wonderful man who takes a couple of days off once
or twice a year to have a look at 200 mouths in order to
inspect 6,000 teeth', was how Vangela Dakis described
the school dentist. [18] Andy Patching is not the school
dentist today, but he is a school governor. In 1996 Dr
Malcolm Moffat, the brother of David Moffat, came out
to Chengelo for six months. He did this for a number of
years and provided medical care for the school. His wife,
Jean, taught English for three days a week.

Ida Waddell performed valuable service as the school
nurse for ten years. Her role has been taken over by Hilda
Tembo from Kasama. Scholastica Kwenda and Richard
Banda are the community nurses for the workers. Ida
Waddell as the school nurse worked for six years without a
doctor in the neighbourhood. She looked after the health
of the pupils and staff members and their families. In
addition she oversaw the work of the Chengelo Workers
Clinic, which at its height served some 1,200 people.
Because Chengelo was in such a remote rural area,
improvisation was often the order of the day. On one
memorable day, she was called at four in the morning
by Michael Bentley. He and Caroline Vidmar (née Nicol)
were on their way to Lusaka as Caroline was expecting

her first child. However, labour pains had come on and it was doubtful if they would make Lusaka. Ida Waddell takes up the story of the birth of baby, Gareth, delivered by lamplight:[19]

*Caroline was ushered through to the Clinic by Ida and Ruth Hill.... Meanwhile Michael and Keith were sent to boil the traditional pots of water, light the fire and fetch the towels. Just at sunrise as the cocks began to crow and the dawn chorus started there came the first cry from Gareth. Since a school clinic does not normally have maternity and neo-natal facilities, the baby was put in the clothes that were brought, wrapped up in a blanket and laid in our daughter's doll's carrycot in front of the wood fire. Mother then headed to Mkushi, since there was a retained placenta to deal with. However the dirt road and the potholes on the Great North Road did the job and admission to Mkushi Hospital was unnecessary. Gareth is now a pupil in the primary school, and he is the only child to have been born at the staff clinic in Chengelo.*

A very serious accident occurred on the 3rd September 2000, when a hot water boiler overheated and exploded at the primary hostel. Four pupils were injured, including one girl, Mwamba Mbewe, who was knocked unconscious with a head injury. She was quickly rushed to the clinic. By God's grace, Dr McAdam, a missionary from North Western Zambia, had been delayed in bringing his son back to school and was still on site. Dr McAdam assisted the school nurses in dealing with the situation. Dr McAdam and Nurse Waddell then drove Mwamba down to Lusaka in a pickup arriving around midnight. It was confirmed that she had fractured her skull and needed emergency treatment, so she was flown down to South Africa. There she made an amazing recovery, without the need for an operation, which doctors said was 'in the order of the miraculous'. God provided gifts to cover all the medical costs with extra to go towards the children's outstanding school fees.

One of the greatest hazards of serving in Africa is journeying by road. On the 12th April 2001, there was a terrible accident involving three UK Chengelo teachers. A coach they were travelling in to South Africa ran into a parked Army truck in Southern Zimbabwe. Seven people died, many were injured, among them Hannah Flanders who lost a leg, Megan Richardson who broke a leg and damaged a knee, and Claire Matthews, who remarkably received only slight injuries. All showed tremendous pluck and fortitude. Hannah Flanders was still teaching at Chengelo in 2004, and was a familiar figure riding her quadbike around the campus. Hannah has a great heart for Africa and at the time of writing (2005) is doing Development Studies in Britain, with a view to returning to Chengelo.

In more recent years, Dr Frank LeBacq at the Tusekelemo Community Medical Centre at Mkushi was available to give back-up support to the nurses at the clinic. Tusekelemo, which literally means, 'We are happy here', was founded in 2001 by Costain and Beatrice Chilala, Barton Young, Don Stacey, Andy and Anne Anderson and a number of other Mkushi farmers with financial support from the Beit Trust. Costain Chilala is a Zambian commercial farmer whose five children all went through Chengelo. Dr LeBacq, a Belgian, has been replaced by a doctor from South Africa.

**The Chengelo Video**
In 2000 a professional video of Chengelo was shown on national television in Zambia. This video had a very favourable response. Amongst the letters received by the Headmaster was this one from a former pupil:
*Dear Mr Richardson,*
*A witness to the light is what Chengelo really is. I was so impressed when I saw the ten-minute promotion video that was shown on TV a couple of days ago. Impressed with the high standard portrayed in every area of life in Chengelo, impressed with the developments since I left, impressed with*

*the continuity of spiritual focus, but most of all impressed with the faithfulness of our God who indeed started the work and is faithful to complete it.*

*To the best of my recollection we started together at Chengelo in 1990, you as the teacher and me as the student. When I think of how it was then and where it is now, I am in awe at what God has done. When you are in the middle of it and progression is continuously taking place around you, you might overlook or fail to see the wonder of his work, but from an outside perspective I can only tell that it looks glorious, and his faithfulness shines through.*

*May God richly bless you, your wife and the school.*

*Sincerely*
*Daniel Pedersen*

**Notes**
[1] *Chengelo: The First Three Years*, p. 39.
[2] Ibid., p. 65.
[3] Ibid., p. 18.
[4] Chesterman's *Bush Telegraph*, March 1992.
[5] *Chengelo: The First Three Years*, p. 54.
[6] Ibid., p. 48.
[7] Ibid., p. 61.
[8] Interview with author, 26th May, 2004.
[9] Interview with author, 26th May, 2004.
[10] See www.chengelo.sch.zm —quick link Chengelocome. to/mkushi.
[11] See above website.
[12] See above website.
[13] See above website.
[14] Email from Waddells to author dated 24.06.05.
[15] Ezzo: *Growing Kid's God's Way*, 1990.
[16] *Handbook for Staff: Discipline Policy Statement.*
[17] Michael Chesterman's *Bush Telegraph*, March 1992.

[18] *Chengelo: The First Three Years*, p. 60.
[19] Email to author dated 23.06.05.

Building the first hostel *May/June 1988*

Men of Mobile Mission Maintenance working on the roof
of the first hostel *July/August 1988*

Building the Solomon Library *December 1997*

The original farmhouse, Lilanda, which became the first boys' hostel, kitchen and dining room *August 1988*

The original classrooms *circa July 1989*

One of the new Design and Technology buildings, designed and built by John Mellen *circa 1999*

Basketball court and sports field   *March 2000*

The swimming pool   *March 2000*

The grandstand overlooking the swimming pool   *September 1998*

A baptismal service in the swimming pool   *November 2000*

Russell and Anne Wyatt *December 1993*

Barton and Yvonne Young *circa July 1989*

David Moffatt with his wife, Christine, sister, Flora,
and brother in law, Robin Pedler *May 2004*

Neil and Ruby Solomon
*End of year 1993*

Portrait of Neil Solomon
in School Library *May 2004*

Tim Sims, Tony Siddle, Ian Richardson, Richard Thornton,
Martin Solomon, Andrew Cowling and Alison Richardson
outside School Library *May 2004*

Graduation day
for the first pupils to go right through the school
with Neil and Ruby Solomon
*December 1993*

A discipleship group in a staff house
*October 2000*

126

An aerial view showing the classrooms,
hostels and sports facilities
—the primary school, the design and technology building,
the library and the new administrative block were not then built
*June 1996*

The official opening ceremony
*May 1993*

# Chapter Seven

# The Resources

'Depend on it! God's work done in God's way will never lack God's provision.' This statement of the great pioneer missionary, Hudson Taylor, was the firm conviction of the founding fathers of Chengelo. David Moffat is unequivocal: 'We have never had to stop developing because of lack of funds.'

Every school requires three basic ingredients: staff, pupils and resources. So far we have traced the provision of the first two elements. So where did all the resources come from? At the outset Chengelo started with minimal resources. It had some land in open bush country miles from the main centres of population in Lusaka and the Copperbelt. It had an old farmhouse, Lilanda, together with its associated buildings. We have seen how the school acquired some old prefabricated classrooms. Besides this there was very little to show on the ground.

## The School Campus[1]
Visitors to the school today will find a superb campus awaiting them at the end of their four-hour drive from Lusaka (see Appendix 2). They will leave the tarmac on the Great North Road and drive along a district road,

which is either dirt or mud according to the season. This leads past Kapanda, now the Wyatts' farm, and then Chimyamauni, the Moffat's farm. The next left turn is marked by an impressive sign on a white wall which indicates the driveway into Chengelo School. Leaving the road which goes on to the Outdoor Centre at Ndubaluba, and the farm belonging to Barton and Yvonne Young, a long drive goes straight into the heart of the school. The drive is adorned with a half-kilometre of flowering trees planted under Barton's direction. If the visitors turn around they will see the long line of the Chilongoma Hills surmounted by a tall wooden cross.

The drive goes past the school farm on the left, and its kitchen garden and orchard on the right. After going through a gate manned by security guards, the visitors enter the campus proper. A road going off to the left leads past the home of the Office Manager and other staff houses, including the home of the Principal. Then comes the amazing green grass of the sportsfield on the left with the squash courts and pitches for cricket, football, rugby, hockey, volleyball and basketball. Then the deep blue of the swimming pool hoves into view with its covered grandstand. Next door are the tennis courts.

On the other side of the road there is the newly established sixth form Centre with its two hostels for boys and girls behind it. The Zambian national flag flies proudly in front of the three classroom blocks standing in a crescent shape. The classrooms look out across the drive towards the new Administration Centre with a central reception area surrounded by its three wings. One wing houses the Principal's and Headteachers' offices, another that of the Office Manager and Accountant and support staff, and a third the staff common room. Behind the Admin Block is the Design and Technology Centre and the road that leads up to Chengelo Primary School.

In front of the Admin Block is the water furrow, which is the lifeblood of the school and its neighbouring farms.

It was dug in the earliest days of the Farm Block on the initiative of Unwin and Sheila Moffat, and draws its water from the Nkolonga River, which joins the Mkushi River on the boundary of Kapanda Farm. Crossing over the furrow by the bridge next to a very handsome stand of tall bamboo trees, the visitors find themselves facing a large roundabout. On their immediate left is the fine library dedicated to the memory of Neil Solomon. Continuing their tour in a clockwise direction they will see the three hostels for Form 5 girls, Senior Girls and Junior Girls. Behind the latter are some more staff houses, the clinic and, further back, the stables. Immediately in front of the visitors are the dining-hall and its associated kitchen block. At the back of the dining-hall and kitchen stand the old farmhouse, Lilanda, and some buildings converted for staff use. The old prefabricated classrooms are still there, but are no longer used for teaching but serve as stores. Three hostels for boys complete the circuit. Beyond the hostels on the south side of the campus is a compound for the school workers.

### Early Costings

Compared with what now exists, the first plans for Chengelo were Lilliputian in their scale. Draft notes for the planned school in 1986 indicate that a capital sum of K38,000 had been raised from within the Fellowship and a further K13,000 from friends of the new school. In addition the farmhouse, land and labour had been provided estimated to the value of some K100,000. It was estimated that a further K150,000 would be required to equip and establish the school. Given that the then exchange rate was in the order of K10 – 12.50 = £1, the Governors were looking to set up their new school on an outlay of some £30,000. But this was predicated on an enrolment of some 16 to 20 pupils! When Peter Green told the founding fathers that they should ratchet up their plans to allow for an annual intake of 50 pupils over five years, leading to a school of 250 pupils, the Governors were being asked to multiply their plans for students by 1250%. It was, to say the least, a tall order. But the Governors bit the bullet, kept their powder dry and trusted in God to provide.

Within a short time the projected costs for the five-year period running up to 1992/3 had mounted to £190,130 for external costs, and K371,900 for internal costs. External costs included staff costs and educational needs, such as textbooks, teaching supplies, and laboratory equipment. Most building costs were internally incurred within Zambia, but some £74,165 was estimated for external purchases.

## Fee Policy

At an early stage the Governors decided that, in order to keep the fees as low as possible, all building and other developments should be funded by donations and grants. Fees were to cover running costs, with 10% of the fees going towards assisted places for children from high priority families whose parents were unable to pay the full fees. It was the aim of the Board that 10% of the children at Chengelo should be assisted by bursaries. In 1997 some 32 children were receiving assistance from bursaries without which they would not have been able to attend Chengelo. Bursaries are awarded by the Headteacher together with a Governor from the Admission and Bursaries Committee. They are awarded solely on the basis of need and merit. The school also charged an enrolment fee, of one term on top of the first term fees, which was allocated to development.

David Moffat admits that fixing the fees in the first term was largely a finger-sucking exercise. They had a small deficit at the end of the first term, so they had to increase the fees for the second term, but there were a lot of hidden subsidies, such as vegetables from Aunty Anne's garden and milk from Russell's dairy. Moreover the prompt payment of fees is often a problem in private schools. At the meeting of the Governors on the 26th January 1991, it was noted that some five families were unable to pay the fees and had been exempted, whilst seven other families had simply failed to pay the fees. Even in 1993 Brian Bentley was appealing in the Chengelo Newsletter for new or secondhand gumboots (sizes 6-10), kitchen and dining hall utensils, tennis racquets and balls, wheelbarrows and small motorbikes.

## Building in Faith

In the early days, there were a number of occasions when David Moffat (in charge of finance) and Russell Wyatt (in charge of the buildings) would stand together and say that if they did not receive some more money by the end of the month they would have to lay workers off, because they did not have enough to pay them. But this never happened. All the early buildings were started on the basis of faith that God would provide the necessary funds to secure their completion. Farmers in the Mkushi Block were very generous and most of the early funds came from within Zambia. At the official opening of the school in May 1993, Russell Wyatt, as Chairman of Governors, stated that 75% of funds came from within Zambia and some 50% of funds from Mkushi. He also said that as at the previous Saturday the school had sufficient funds in the building account to purchase just eight bags of cement, but the work would go on. The school has never had to borrow money, except on a very short-term basis when it was known for certain where the repayment funds were coming from.

The Governors were fortunate in that two of their number, David Moffat and Barton Young, were members of the Boards of Barclays and Grindlays (now Stanbic) Banks respectively. David Moffat was also a member of the Zambian Investment Board and the Northern Zambian Correspondent of the Beit Trust. Both banks and the Beit Trust gave financial assistance to the school. Grindlays helped with money for the dining-hall. The Beit Trust gave a £20,000 grant for science equipment, and other monies in tranches, as well as putting up £50,000 for the library. BP provided solar lighting for some of the hostels. The British High Commission gave a grant of £6,000 for the purchase of IBM compatible computers. The Schimmelpennick-Campbell Education Trust gave grants for books and other educational requirements. In addition, support came to the school from friends overseas. Michael Chesterman opened a bank account for the Trust in England. Traugott Hartmann used his extensive contacts with churches and missionary societies in Germany.[2]

Latterly the school received a number of significant grants from organisations. The European Union Microprojects programme gave K1m for hostel development and later money for water development. Europe also provided 13,000 kg of tinned food, which enabled Chengelo to feast on such exotic treats as tinned prunes and Argentinian corned beef. Many of these items were shipped out from Britain by Medical Missionary News (MMN), a Brethren organisation, which supplied the Brethren (Christian Missions in Many Lands) mission stations on the Beloved Strip.

The man behind MMN is Norman Lane, who owns a firm called Norman's Taps and Dyes Ltd, which is run from a warehouse on the outskirts of London. In addition to producing Medical Missionary News, he collects items to be shipped out to Brethren missionary stations throughout the world. All items for Chengelo can be sent through his organisation. Many donations are made by individuals as well as by groups. At one time a large amount of tins of unlabelled food was supplied, which variously yielded fruit, soup and tinned meats. Among other donations were sewing machines, typewriters, clothes and bicycles. These items were kept in the admin store before distribution. One morning a staff member asked Keith Rushby, who looked after the stores, if she might have a bicycle. Keith was surprised to learn that she had been born with only one hand, which meant that she could only use her right hand. In addition she wanted a bicycle with straight handlebars. They went to the store and the first bicycle inspected had straight handlebars and the brake and gear controls all on the right side. God had provided precisely for her needs as he provided so richly for the school in other ways.

In 1998, Ian Richardson, now the Headmaster, wrote in the Chengelo *Newsletter* that, 'The pace of development has hardly slackened at all over the past ten years. We now have eight hostels, fifteen classrooms, three laboratories, twenty five staff houses, a dining hall, kitchens, stables, swimming pool, squash courts, grandstand and administration block. In addition the Training Farm has grown rapidly with a pig sty and pens, poultry houses, dairy parlour, milk shed and slaughter house, and these are situated next door to our building and mechanical workshops. Most recently the Neil Solomon Memorial Library, which is our latest project, has just been completed.'[3] At this stage the five-year development plan envisaged the construction of an Art, Design and Technology Centre, a new primary school and a new Sixth Form Centre. It was also hoped to build a school hall with a combined gymnasium and assembly hall. In the providence of God all but the school hall has been built.

## The Library

The school library started life in the old prefab, classroom 3. It had approximately 500 books that had been donated by individuals and by the Country Club. Mrs Pietersen, assisted by Mpande Simumba, was the first librarian. At the end of 1989 the library was moved to what had been the dining-room in the old farmhouse, Lilanda. There the library grew with more acquisitions. Christine Moffat's parents, Mr and Mrs Sewell, introduced the Dewey Classification System, and then Mrs Parker-Dennison catalogued the whole library. At the same time a small Christian library had been established thanks to the donation of some books from Mr and Mrs Beardsell, who ran a mobile Christian book service in the UK.

On the tenth anniversary of the school, the Neil Solomon Memorial Library was officially dedicated by Ruby (Braumann) Solomon, who travelled up from South Africa with Timothy and Luke for the occasion. The fine new library with a splendid portrait of Neil Solomon, painted by Axel Braumann, in its foyer, has a capacity for 13,000 lending books and over 5,000 reference books. The anniversary weekend also saw the opening of the new computer room. At a thanksgiving service attended by nearly five hundred people on the Sunday, David Moffat challenged everyone to work out the vision of Chengelo, confident in the faithfulness of God who had provided so abundantly over the first ten years.

## The Chengelo Educational Trust
Major assistance to the work of the school has come from the Chengelo Educational Trust (CET). The Governors considered that it would be helpful to have a British-based registered trust which could help with fund-raising, as well as interviewing potential staff, stimulating prayer support and possibly assisting in the procurement of supplies in the United Kingdom. An inaugural meeting was held at Partnership House, Waterloo Road, London, on the 27th September 1991. At the meeting, Peter Green was elected Chairman, the Revd Norman Wyatt became Secretary, and Michael Chesterman, who had been operating a bank account for the school, became Treasurer. Others at the meeting were Bob Baker, Nigel Roe, the Revd John Symons, and Elizabeth (Liz) Blake, the daughter of Russell and Anne Wyatt. Southampton, Bath and Bristol were identified as areas of potential support. An open Fellowship Day was arranged for the 6th June 1992 at Widcombe Baptist Church, Bath.

In January 1993 the first of numerous meetings of the CET was held at Zambia House, 2 Palace Gate, London. The trust members were welcomed by the High Commissioner, Mr Love Mtesa. That year the sum of £6,964.01 was transferred from an account held in England by Mkushi Christian Fellowship to CET, thus providing the Trust with a financial launch pad for its future work. The Trust then began to receive a number of private gifts, including some for pupils' school fees. In that year the Trust made its first substantial donation of £5,000 for science equipment at the school. In 1995 the Trust paid out more than £27,000 to the school, of which the largest item was £12,500 for the school farm as well as £2,000 for the water supply. With the help of European Microprojects money, water was now drawn directly from the Mkushi River and not from the furrow. The Parent Teachers Association raised K20m for the filtration and chlorination system, to which sum the CET added £5,000 in 1996. Earlier the Lusaka PTA had raised K1.2m from a bridge evening to help pay for the grandstand by the pool.

In 1997 the Trust set up a fund which was initially to go towards re-settling qualifying, long-serving, school staff. This has subsequently been merged into the bursary fund, the total of which has reached £100,000. The CET has committed itself to make available to the school a regular sum of money to be used to enable deserving pupils to be given assisted places or bursaries. In 1998, the Trust Treasurer, who was now Robin Pedler, the husband of Flora, David Moffat's sister, reported that fund income for the year had topped £20,000 for the first time. In 2000 the Trust's charitable income reached a record £56,401. Robin later commented that from a management point of view, the school's ability to deliver on a plan was remarkable. He had never experienced such a full performance as they had achieved for their 1998 – 2002 plan. This was the more striking, in that most planners believe they know where the funding is coming from to support their projects, whereas Chengelo proceeds in faith, which underlines the importance of fund-raising!

The latest CET accounts for 2003 show an income of £30,158, of which £13,709 went to the school directly and £14,000 went to the gratuity and bursary funds. In 2001 25% of children were on asssisted places, 10.7% of pupils were the children of missionaries, and 12.6% of pupils were the children of Zambian full-time Christian workers. Robin and Flora Pedler were very active in fund raising for the school and held a number of concerts, tennis competitions, and other events in aid of Chengelo in their home town of Beaconsfield.

Another successful fund-raising venture was that organised by Michael Chesterman to provide a tractor for the school farm. In 2000 he started collecting money to pay for a Massey Ferguson 290. The need was advertised at various agricultural shows and amongst various Norfolk churches. Considerable progress towards the target of £10,000 was made, but then the project seemed to stall, Michael went down to London for the baptism of his granddaughter. In the church car park there were lots of expensive cars. In the church Michael spotted a plain wooden box.

"'What's that for?"

"Oh, it's our Lazarus box, for special projects in aid of the poor."

"And what project are you currently sponsoring?"

"Oh, we've just finished one, and are looking for another."

Of course you can guess what happened —by Christmas the tractor was paid for and on its way.'[4]

For Michael this was one of his TLWP (The Lord Will Provide) moments.

When Norman Wyatt stood down in January 1995 as Secretary of the CET, Bob Baker was elected to take his place. Bob was then Headteacher at Valentines High School, in Ilford, Essex, a failing comprehensive, which he successfully turned around. Bob, acting on behalf of Chengelo, had taken an important role in interviewing potential staff members for the school. He visited the school on a number of occasions, and in May 2004 succeeded in drawing together a party of thirteen members of CET to visit Chengelo School. In addition to Bob, 'the Baker's Dozen' included Flora and Robin Pedler, a number of relatives of Russell Wyatt, and Rosemary Goulding, who had actively raised money for the school with her stand at the Ross-on-Wye Festival. The school laid on a full programme of activities for the visitors, which included visits to Ndubaluba, the workers' compound and the school farm. The party was also involved in the evenings with discipleship groups, supper with the 6th and 5th Form pupils and career talks.

**Food for the School**
In the early days of Chengelo, much of the fresh food was provided by local farmers. In addition to his three weekly visits to Ndola to buy food, Keith Rushby would go once a week to Mkushi to buy eggs from Mr Parshotam and Mrs Arnautovic. Vegetables would come from a number of local farmers, such as the Andersons, the Nicolls, the Staceys, and the Cantlays, as well as the Wyatts, Moffats and Youngs. Some vegetables were grown on site, where Tennison Simfukwe, the caretaker for the Moffats at Lilanda, transformed its enlarged garden. Meat would come from the Youngs, Moffats or Wyatts, and chickens from the Parshotams. Occasionally Chengelo would get some pork or other foods donated by one of the school parents. An attempt to encourage pupils to develop their own vegetable plots was not successful. They were each given a square metre plot to grow maize, beans and other vegetables. Sadly, a cow found its way into the plots and ate all the maize. But field trips to local farms, such as the Shrosbrees' tobacco or the Staceys' tomatoes, were a regular part of the school diary.

## The School Farm

But inevitably the question began to be asked, why does Chengelo not have its own farm, which could both feed the school and be a model training farm for agricultural science subjects? A school farm had always been on the Governors' development agenda. Funding was the main brake on the venture, and a sustained effort was made to find a donor for the farm. A great deal of work was done at the Chengelo end in preparing an application to the European Union. Hours were spent in filling out the necessary forms. The paperwork was passed on to Dr Peter Green, the Chairman of CET, who applied formally on behalf of the school. But it proved very difficult to meet the EU's criteria for funding, and in due course the application was turned down.

A number of very substantial gifts from private individuals enabled the farm project to get under way. In 1994, Michael Chesterman, then Treasurer of the Chengelo Educational Trust, put in an application to Bread for the World ('Brot fur die Welt'), a large German mission agency. The application was sent in August to the head office in Stuttgart. No reply was received. A polite reminder was submitted. But by Christmas there was still no reply. So Michael decided to take the bull by the horns. He booked a flight to Stuttgart and asked for an appointment on 6th January for himself and Traugott Hartmann, a school Governor, who was then on leave in Germany. The day dawned. It was biting cold. Michael and Traugott turned up at the Bread for the World offices, to find them closed. 'Heute geschlossen' – closed today. It was Epiphany, a public holiday.

There was nothing for it but to swallow the disappointment and fly home empty-handed. The delay continued without any apparent progress. Then, on the 27th March 1995, Michael got a surprise telephone call.

"Mr. Chesterman?"

"Yes."

"This is Mr Hess —the man you never met! I am pleased to inform you that our Allocation Board has approved an amount of DM50,000 for the Chengelo Training Farm."

Michael's reaction: 'Wow! Fifty thousand marks —that's over £20,000! Praise the Lord!'

The German grant together with the individual donations and that of £12,500 from CET put the establishment of the farm on a firm basis.

Tony Siddle came from Chimfunshi Ranch, near the Congo border and some 70 kilometres from Chingola, to develop the farm. The farm covers 70 hectares of land and employs some 20 permanent workers. There are two hectares of mixed vegetables and two hectares of orchards with oranges, lemons, mulberries, guavas, pawpaws and mangoes. When the author visited Chengelo with the CET members in May 2004, the visitors were shown around the farm by Tony Siddle.

We admired the dairy cows, which are the progeny of eight cows given to the school in its first year by Bill Hart, a longtime friend of Russell Wyatt. Bill Hart was dying of cancer at the time. He would certainly be thrilled to see how his generous gift is now providing Chengelo with its daily milk supply. Until the Chengelo farm was developed, the little herd was held on the Wyatt's farm for five years. When it moved across to the school there were 25 cows and heifer calves. The cows have been bred over the years to the point where they are nearly pure Jersey. The Jerseys are not such high producers of milk as the Friesians or the Holsteins, but they are much tougher and able to cope with a more varied food diet. The farm is hand-milking about 30 cows and the average daily production is about 12.7 litres per cow, and goes up to about 15 litres in season. This is more milk than the school requires, so the farm is making butter right through the year, and giving the surplus milk to the pigs. For meat, the farm buys in finished steers and slaughters about three a week for school consumption. The farm has a couple of draught oxen, which are trained to the voice and are a familiar sight pulling a cart around the farm.

The farm has an eight-sow unit for its large white pigs. The sows are served by the boar, and generally produce two litters a year. They go into the farrowing house until the piglets are weaned at about five weeks. Litters average about twelve piglets but can go as high as fifteen. The farm produces its own bacon, sausages and other pork products.

The farm also has high-producing chicken hybrids for its egg consumption, which is roughly 300 to 400 eggs a day. Rather than using a battery system, the chickens have the run of deep litter in the chicken house. This gives them more freedom but also allows them to eat their own eggs or even each other. For this reason they are debeaked, and cannibalism can usually be rectified by a change in the diet. The chickens and pigs are all fed by soft food from the farm. A wonderful fifty-year old Paxman engine, bought for some £50 and still in good working order, is used for milling maize. Mealie meal for the workers is purchased locally.

The butchery was built with funds provided by CET at a cost of some £10,000 – £12,000. Funds were also boosted by a private donation. Philip and Betty Sercombe searched the length and breadth of England to find the requisite equipment for the butchery. This equipment was then despatched to Zambia by the Sercombes, who were funded by the Yapton Fellowship in West Sussex. The meat is hung in the cold room for about a week, but the room is cold enough for the meat to be hung for up to two or three weeks, if necessary. The compressor can now be run directly off the mains electricity and does not depend as formerly on a generator. The meat is cut up in the processing room. Friday, the driver, is a versatile man who can drive, cut meat and make butter. Excellent rump steak is bought by visitors and parents for £2.50 a kilo, which about a quarter of its cost in England. The farm aims to make a modest profit, which it has succeeded in doing for the last few years. The big current need is to build a proper slaughterhouse to replace the existing outdoor slaughter slab and gantry.

When the farm was set up it had a three-fold purpose. It aimed: (i) to supply fresh produce to feed the school; (ii) to provide a practical base for those pupils studying agricultural science in their IGCSE exams; (iii) to reach out into the local community by opening the farm to small-scale peasant farmers to share knowledge and ideas. The first aim has been fully met as is evidenced in the excellent food served in the school dining room. It was Keesjan van der Maas from Holland who introduced agriculture to the curriculum and made it one of the most popular and successful subjects. His wife, Carla, was a houseparent in the junior girls' hostel, and both Mr and Mrs van der Maas made a most significant contribution to the musical life of the school during their five year stay. In latter years a lot of Tony Siddle's time has been devoted to the outreach work of the farm.

**Agricultural Outreach**
The farm has been running field days for peasant farmers and bringing them on to the farm to see how it is operated. Now the work is mainly taking place in the villages where ten demonstration plots have been set up. These plots are little modules showing conservation tillage, crop rotation and some agro-forestry, as well as the encouragement of organic farming. A system known as minimum tillage is used. This was developed by a Christian farmer in Zimbabwe, who devised it for the use of hoes and the avoidance of ploughing. Almost invariably the peasant farmers are late in planting their maize because they have to wait for the rains before they can plough. With minimum tillage, small holes are dug in August, to which are added small cupfuls of fertilisers and the required number of maize seeds. This system

allows the farmer to get well prepared before the rains come, and to concentrate his efforts on weeding. It has been calculated that a quarter of a hectare of maize (one lima) if properly grown is enough to feed a family for a year. Some farmers have produced up to 36 x 50 kilo bags off one lima. The idea is to rotate the maize crop with a legume, such as sun hemp, and then a root crop such as sweet potatoes. With one hectare of land the farmer can have two legumes, maize and a root crop. By removing sweet potatoes from the rotation, another cereal crop can be introduced. Although the government is now providing seeds and fertilisers instead of loans for peasant farmers, these often come late and cannot be relied upon. This is why organic means of production are being encouraged.

### Switched On

In the CET *Newsletter* of July 2003, the Principal announced a new chapter in the life of Chengelo. 'After many years of faithful prayers and not inconsiderable lobbying, a significant milestone in the life of the school was announced with the switching on of the mains electricity on 11 April.' Whilst the advent of electric power was generally welcomed, there were some who mourned the passing of an era. 'There was something romantic about enjoying the candle-light and conversing with other night-owl friends after the generator went off.'[5]

In 2002, Peter Green, the Chairman of the Chengelo Educational Trust, paid a two-week visit to the school. He reported in the Newsletter: 'As I walked around the clean, orderly campus, I reflected on my forty years' experience of working in Africa and in hundreds of schools around the world and I wondered where I had seen such care given to the environment. As I observed lessons I wondered where I had seen such care given to learning, and to pupils. My wife visited the residential hostels and there she found a relaxed and friendly atmosphere. It was all very impressive.'[6]

**Notes**
[1] See Appendix 2 for the plan of the campus.
[2] Analysis of donations as at the 10th May 1992 showed the total cost of Chengelo as K21,245,000 funded by:

| Farmers – | | |
|---|---|---|
| Mkushi Christian Fellowship | 10,610,000 | 49.9% |
| Farmers – Others | 3,646,000 | 17.1% |
| EEC Microprojects | 2,000,000 | 9.4% |
| Student Registration Fees | 1,604,000 | 7.6% |
| Private Individual Donations | 1,175,000 | 5.5% |
| ANZ Grindlays Bank | 500,000 | 2.4% |
| Mkushi Christian Fellowship | 441,000 | 2.1% |
| Parents (not included in fees) | 380,000 | 1.8% |
| Beit Trust | 300,000 | 1.4% |
| Parent Teachers Association | 291,000 | 1.4% |
| Companies | 198,000 | 0.9% |
| Barclays Bank | 100,000 | 0.5% |
| Total | 21,245,000 | 100.00% |

In addition the following had given bursaries: Barclays Bank (3.5 places, K1,080,250), ANZ Grindlays Bank (1 place, K318,000), plus private individuals and charitable organisations (8 places).
The figures of donations include donations in kind, e.g. tractor time, lorry time etc.
[3] *Newsletter*, No. 8, 1998
[4] Correspondence to the author from Michael Chesterman dated 15.12.03.
[5] Keith and Ida Waddell in e-mail to author dated 23.06.05.
[6] *Chengelo Educational Trust Newsletter*, No 16, 2002.

# Chapter Eight

# The Primary School

## A School for Staff Children

Chengelo has had a primary school from the beginning, since the children of staff members needed schooling. Initially the small number of staff children were taught by Ruby Solomon, but later Ruby was able to hand over this responsibility to Norma Grenzenberg, a former Treverton colleague. This released Ruby Solomon to teach biology and music at the secondary school. Mrs Mbozi also helped with the primary children.

Alison Richardson came out with her husband in August 1990, having met Neil Solomon on a visit to Bristol. They were on a two-year contract, but stayed for fourteen years, apart from two whole terms out on long leave. Alison's first job at Chengelo was to teach the staff children. At that time there were about twelve of primary school age, ranging from five to twelve. This tiny school was held in the old farmhouse. During Alison's first couple of years, some of the local farming block children were admitted to Chengelo because the parents could not find a suitable primary school nearby, and the only alternative was to send them off to boarding school. The parents approached Chengelo and asked if their children might be admitted as day pupils or weekly boarders. So the little primary class was increased with another five or six local children. As there were then no boarding facilities, the children were lodged with different families. The Richardsons had two children staying with them for a while, in addition to their own little ones. In 1992, when the Allens arrived at Chengelo, and Alison Richardson went home to have her first baby, Angie Allen took over the work of teaching the staff primary school children.

In his report of the 5th March1991, Dr Peter Green had advocated the idea of a single stream junior school for 8 to 11 year olds, a total of 100 children, leading into the secondary school. Dr Green gave his opinion that in some ways junior education was more important than secondary education. When Michael Chesterman, acting as an educational consultant in 1991, considered this proposal, he felt that the physical restraints on buildings and the increased cost factors militated against this expansion. He therefore recommended to the Governors that Chengelo should remain essentially a secondary school with a small primary facility for staff children on an ad hoc basis split into an upper and lower primary.

For some two years the Fellowship sought in prayer to discern whether a primary school was part of God's plan for the school and in keeping with the original vision. The pressure from the parents was not only for Chengelo to establish a full primary school, but also to move into sixth form education. The Board of Governors was agreed that these developments should not go ahead until the Fellowship was convinced that these moves really were 'of the Lord.' Although some parents were keen for Chengelo to open a primary school, the Headmaster told parents in the Newsletter dated 10th June 1994 that the response was inadequate for the school to go ahead.

## Keith and Ida Waddell

Keith and Ida Waddell arrived at Chengelo in August 1994 and stayed ten years. They had worked in Zimbabwe for three years, and answered an advertisement in the *Times Educational Supplement* for a primary teacher and a registered general nurse at Chengelo. They found some 27 primary pupils divided into an infant and junior class, housed in two rooms in the old Lilanda farmhouse, which also served as the school library. In December 1994 Keith was appointed Acting-Head of Chengelo Primary School.

During Keith's time as Acting Head, the primary school moved from a mainly staff and local facility with some weekly boarders to an autonomous fully-fledged primary school with a nation-wide catchment. This was in response to the need set out in the 1994 Primary School Development Plan, following Peter Green's recommendations, for the provision of primary education of a similar quality and standard to the secondary school. Academically it would prepare pupils for the secondary school and share the vision of Chengelo 'as a witness to the light.'[1]

In January 1995 the primary school moved from the farmhouse to three prefabricated huts, vacated by the secondary school following the completion of the secondary classroom block. The primary now consisted of three composite classes: an Infant, Middle and Upper. But the primary school had not attained autonomy and was still regarded as a department of the secondary school. This caused some tension when decisions were made without adequate consultation and imposed in a top-down manner. However, following the resignation of Brian Mather as Headmaster, the management structure of the whole school was reorganised. The school Executive Committee was abolished and replaced by a Senior Management Team, and the primary school was given a voice at all levels of management.

Melvyn Nolan took over from Keith Waddell at the end

of 1995. Soon after he arrived, Melvyn wanted to be shown around the Ropes Course. He thought that he would try it out for himself and all went well until he reached the trapeze. He failed to grab the rope at the other side and had to let go of the swing and drop the four or five feet to the ground. He landed awkwardly on his ankle and pulled the ligaments. A wheelchair was quickly summoned and Melvyn was rushed to the clinic. For Keith Waddell this was a learning experience as a deputy. 'Never mind the job description, your first duty is to keep your Head out of trouble.'[2]

## Melvyn and Julie Nolan

Melvyn Nolan and his wife Julie came out in November 1995 and stayed until March 2002. Melvyn was an experienced headmaster of some fifteen years standing in Britain. Both Melvyn and Julie, who was also a teacher of both primary and secondary pupils, took early retirement to come out to Chengelo. Melvyn first learnt about Chengelo through a colleague who had heard Roy Fellowes, the father-in-law of Ian Richardson, speaking about the school at a conference at Lee Abbey. The Chengelo Governors were wanting to expand the primary education into a full-blown school and the Nolans had all the requisite background for this. Melvyn describes his first impressions of Chengelo: 'It was a lovely surprise. I got there thinking that I was going to darkest Africa. When I walked into the primary school then held in the old prefab huts, I thought to myself, "My goodness, I could be in a school in England." I recognised books and displays on the wall and the good teaching that was going on, and I thought, "I could be redundant out here."'[3]

## Chengelo Primary School Opens, 8th January 1996

On 8th January 1996, Chengelo Primary School came properly into being with Melvyn Nolan as Headmaster. Keith Waddell was the deputy Headmaster. Philip and

Anne Elledge, who had both taught in Lebanon, became the primary houseparents. With the construction of the primary hostel there was now capacity for some 60 pupils by the end of the first term.

Far from being redundant, Melvyn Nolan had to play a key role as the primary school expanded and finally moved into its purpose-built premises. In this time the school expanded from three or four classes to one with seven grades. Melvyn had not been at the school more than one or two days when he was taken over to have a look at what is now the Zambezi hostel. 'I was told by Brian Mather, the Head, "You have to make the decision, Mr Nolan, whether we take boarders into this hostel in January 1996." I looked at it, having been in Africa for two days, and said, "How do you expect me to make that decision?" I would hasten to add that the roof was not yet on. I said, "I will make that decision at the end of the month when I have seen how fast the workers actually work." We did make a decision that we would take boarders in at the end of that month. But a lot of prayer went into that building, especially over the roof that was coming up from South Africa, and had not actually arrived.'

Work proceeded on the construction of the new primary site. As the day loomed for the opening of the new school, disaster struck. 'Suddenly a whirlwind came through the school and took off the roof of the secondary school library computer room, and hit two of our new classrooms and wrapped up the tin roof as if it was silver paper. That was a bit of a shock. You then saw the quality of Zambian workers, who obviously like crises. They got to work and put the roof back on within two or three hours, and worked after it was dark at 18.00 into the night, and made sure that the rains did not get in. It was a shock to have one's lovely new school roof ripped off. It was amazing that nobody was actually injured. If we had had children around they would have been decapitated.'

The primary school, despite being on the same campus

as the secondary, tried to maintain its own ethos. Rules drawn up for the secondary school proved inappropriate for younger children. Chengelo had a rule of no physical contact between the sexes. This was hard to explain to a five-year old boy who wanted to walk hand in hand with a friend who happened to be a girl. How did they cope with these rules? 'We tended to ignore them', was Melvyn's blunt reply, adding, 'Of course we discussed it together.'

Melvyn found that the most satisfying thing about teaching at Chengelo was that the children actually wanted to learn. 'They were lovely to teach. I had been a head for fifteen years, and we had gone through the national curriculum introduction and all that meant: the upheaval that affected primary much more than secondary. As soon as they were going to test in secondary schools, the teachers objected and they stopped —initially. But for primary they kept moving the goalposts, so you got very dissatisfied staff, and this had an effect upon the children. The culture and the climate in the UK are everybody has rights but nobody seems to have responsibilities. You could have in primary schools, six, seven and eight-year olds saying, "This is my right", and not being prepared to take on any responsibility themselves for their own learning. Sometimes in England teaching could be quite difficult, and you sometimes had children who did not really want to be in school and could be quite disruptive.'

There were, of course, frustrations in working at Chengelo. Melvyn cited the total absence of supply teachers, which posed problems when staff were sick and meant that others would somehow have to cover the gaps. Then there was knowing that any equipment ordered could take up to six months to arrive. This required enormous patience. There was the constant pressure of being on call for twenty-four hours a day. Community living also posed stresses and strains, in a situation where everybody knew exactly what everybody else was doing. People worked, socialised and worshipped with the same group of people. A teacher could find herself in a home group meeting and wanting to open up her heart, when she was sitting in the same room as her head of department, the Headmaster and possibly the Chairman of Governors. At times it all felt a bit like living in a hothouse.

Looking back over his six and a half years at Chengelo, Melvyn could see how there had been a general improvement all round. 'It was interesting looking at all the productions that we did over the years. In our very last term we finished up with doing a cantata, *Resurrection Rock*, conducted by Amy Bishop, a student volunteer. It was interesting to compare that with our very first cantata, called *The Trojan War*, and just seeing how the standard had improved over those six-and-a-half years. Same sort of children, but we now had tradition, the fact that they were used to doing these things and it was part of their normal way of life in the school. I am sure that the school will have grown and gone on since we left.'

## John and Ruth Mellen

John Mellen took a major role in the design and the construction of the new primary school facility. John and his wife, Ruth, were at Chengelo for five years from December 1994 to December 1999. Ruth got involved in managing the Zongwe Hostel with 21 primary children. After one year she became houseparent of the newly built Zambezi Hostel, catering for 54 primary boarders. In her last year she went back to run the refurbished Zongwe Hostel with some 24 pupils. John came to Chengelo to teach maths, and later introduced design technology and technical drawing into the curriculum. He taught development studies in his final year at the school.

In addition to his teaching, John utilised his 25 years' previous experience in the building industry as a qualified engineer. He found himself heavily involved in the implementation of three schemes which had already been designed. So it was John who oversaw the construction of a water filtration plant, a foul drainage development and the Zambezi Hostel for primary children. Then John turned his attention to the new Solomon Memorial Library, which had been designed by John Thornberry, an architect, who was at Chengelo for a while. Later, John was responsible for the design and construction of the fifth form girls' hostel, the Design and Technology Centre, and the enlargement to Zongwe Hostel. His crowning achievement was the building of the new primary school. He writes: 'We both felt that coming to Chengelo, when other maths teachers were leaving and at a time of a new building phase, was confirmation that we were there at the time of God's choosing. The five years were very full ones, but we would not have missed the experience for anything.'[4] Since returning to England, the Mellens, as regional representatives in East Anglia, have been very active in raising money for the Chengelo Educational Trust.

## The New Primary School Facility Opens
## 17th March 2000

The pressure on space had meant that it had become imperative to build brand-new classroom facilities for the primary school. A decision was taken to proceed with the work in 1997. In 1999, building began on the classroom block. The completion of this building freed-up space for the newly started sixth form.

The grand opening of the new primary school facility was on the 17th March 2000. After two weeks of heavy showers the school was blessed with a fine day for the thanksgiving service and the official opening ceremony. The whole school, primary, secondary and sixth form, came together with Governors, parents and friends. The primary recorder group led the singing of the National Anthem, followed by the school song, 'Witness to the Light'. Russell Wyatt, the Chairman of the Board of

Governors, reminded the audience of how the Board and the Mkushi Christian Fellowship had sought the will of God at each stage of the school's expansion. He believed that this new development seemed fully in line with God's will for Chengelo.

The special guest of honour for the occasion was Mrs Anne Kapolyo, herself a primary school teacher and a school parent with two daughters at Chengelo. Mrs Kapolyo defined the purpose of primary education as 'trying to meet the children's needs, encouraging them to live fully while gaining understanding in literacy, numeracy and in the social expectations of society'.[5] She stressed the essential role that parents play in giving their children emotional security. 'Let them know that you love them, say it and show it, give them some of your time.' She emphasised that purpose-built classrooms are not essential but that 'the secure climate of trust is greatly enhanced in this new environment.'

Before unveiling the commemorative plaque, dedicating the primary school 'To The Glory of God', Mrs Kapolyo focused on the principal purpose of Chengelo. It is 'a light shining out in this community and all over Zambia, arising to draw people to Jesus. May the light of good news shine from Chengelo Primary School in education in this country, seeing the potential in each child, encouraging the weak academically to give their best and praising and rewarding effort as much as achievement.'

After the service the guests enjoyed walking around the new complex of buildings and admiring the work of the children. The day was a wonderful opportunity for everybody to see the results of John Mellen's designs, and both his hard work and that of the builders in bringing them to fruition.

The new complex consists of classrooms for each one of the seven grades. These classrooms are built in a rectangle around the central play area. In addition there is a primary hall and a primary library, a primary admin block and staff room. There is also a special needs room. Initially Lin Carter was responsible for looking after children with special needs, but in the last couple of years, Naomi Cowling, who has had experience with special needs children in the UK, has taken over from Lin. The special needs provision has led to more enquiries from parents. There are a lot of language problems and some children have slight dyslexia. Also some children may have particular problems in numeracy.

## Alison Richardson

In May 2004, the primary school had 101 children. Of these pupils, 36 were the children of teachers or administrative staff. 44 children were termly boarders, and 16 were weekly boarders. All the boarders are now accommodated in two primary hostels. There are four or five day pupils whose parents live on the Farming Block at a distance of about twenty minutes' drive. The headmistress at the time of writing is Alison Richardson, but she is standing down. At the time of writing, it has been announced that Alison is to be succeeded by Mr Steve Jordan.[6] As she looked back on her time in the primary school, Alison said:

*The biggest joy are the children. In the UK I was teaching in quite a rough school with lots of social needs. Coming here you find the children are far more enthusiastic about school and keen to learn, and they get excited about coming to school, even though it is a boarding school away from home, and you see quite a lot of improvement —not just in their education, but in their attitudes and behaviour. In their own Christian faith you see great developments, which is really exciting. Working as a team is something that has given me a lot of pleasure in the last two years. The staff come from all sorts of different church backgrounds, some from UK and some from Zambia.*

*A lot of the frustrations come from being so isolated. You cannot always get what you want quickly. Living in community, 50% or more of the time is really nice, but there are times when you find that you are all living on top of each other and it is not easy to get away. Things happen and you are living on site and you deal with them. You are officially on duty twenty-four hours a day, which is very different from most places in the UK.*

*When I first came out, I was frightened of the dark and the spiders and the snakes. I think that as a couple we have adapted together as most of our married life has now been in Zambia. Our families are back in the UK, but both of our parents have been out two or three times. That helped them because I think that they were imagining the worst. My parents actually came out here and worked as houseparents for four years, which was really good, because it was just after Daniel was born, so both of our children have grown up quite close to my parents, and know them as grandparents and have a good relationship with them.*[7]

## What Makes Chengelo Primary So Special?

What then makes Chengelo Primary so special? The Chengelo *Newsletter* sought to answer that question in its December 2000 issue.

*Chengelo Primary, like the secondary, is first and foremost a Christian school, where the aim is for children to come to a personal knowledge of God and to have a relationship with him. We aim to teach a Christian world-view so that the children begin to understand the world around them and form a Christian perspective. All the termly boarders attend a lively Sunday school called King's Kids and many also attend the optional discipleship classes held after school.*

*A recent visitor to the school was amazed at the happy, secure and caring environment in the primary hostels. This provides the children with the ideal base to grow and develop at school. Despite missing home, the children soon find extra 'brothers' and 'sisters' as they build friendships with other children. The role of the live-in houseparent is crucial in helping the children to settle in. Rather than using large dormitories, the children sleep in bedrooms and are expected to keep their own area tidy. They are encouraged to be aware of the needs of others as they live together.*

*You have only to look in one of the classrooms to see that the lessons are exciting and fun. The walls are bright and colourful and the displays light and airy. Most rooms have a carpeted area enabling a lot of close interactive work between the teacher and the class.*

*There is always a lot of practical activity going on and there is a great emphasis on understanding and the application of knowledge. Recently one class made a full size Egyptian reed boat; others designed musical instruments using hand tools and some designed their own clay pots. All classrooms have their own computer to support the classroom teaching. Children are encouraged to read widely. Each class has its own library and the children also have access to the school library.*

*The primary children have over fifteen clubs on offer to them after school. Sport features highly and recent highlights for the girls included a trip to Musikili School in Mazabuka to play netball and hockey. The boys also have had several football matches against local schools. Some children's talents lie in the arts. A range of activities is also available to them, including recorders, piano, a music group, crafts, sewing and drama. There is also a science and environment club. A few weeks ago a crocodile appeared in a nearby dam giving children the opportunity to see some real wildlife. 'Is it real?' one child asked.*[8]

**Notes**

[1] There was some sensitivity as to whether Chengelo's Primary would be seen as being in direct competition with Sakeji School, the long established Brethren missionary school in Mwinilunga district. Sakeji had an excellent reputation but its position, in the far north-west corner of Zambia, meant that it was very remote and a very long drive for parents living in Lusaka or down south.

[2] Email to author dated 23.06.05.
[3] Interview with author, 24.04.04.
[4] Note to author dated 21.11.04.
[5] *Chengelo Educational Trust Newsletter*, No. 12, July 2000.
[6] *Imbila*, July 2004.
[7] Interview with author, 18.05.04.
[8] *Chengelo Educational Trust Newsletter*, No. 17, December 2002.

# Chapter Nine

# The Mind

## The International General Certificate of Secondary Education

A letter dated 8th December 1988 from the Ministry of General Education gave Chengelo its long awaited official government recognition as a private secondary school. From the first, Chengelo decided to prepare its pupils for a new educational qualification called the International General Certificate of Secondary Education (IGCSE). This had been recommended by Dr Peter Green in his foundational report dated 1st December 1987. In his opinion the IGCSE discouraged rote learning and encouraged concept formation and development. Chengelo was one of the first schools in Africa to subscribe to the Cambridge IGCSE, which was designed for a wider ability range than the GCE Ordinary Level exams. Although it was intended to accommodate varying levels of achievement, the IGCSE also maintained the standard of GCE Ordinary Level and School Certificate examinations. The higher grades awarded in IGCSE have direct comparability with those awarded for GCE Ordinary Level, and with the General Certificate of Secondary Education, used in the United Kingdom. To allow candidates of differing skills to show their capabilities, differentiated papers and/or questions are set for most subjects so that assessment appropriate to a wide ability range is provided.

In Years 1 and 2 pupils follow a basic curriculum similar to that used in Grades 8 and 9 within the Zambian state system. In Year 3 more specific preparation is given for the IGCSE syllabus. Then in Years 4 and 5 the IGCSE syllabus is followed leading up to the writing of the IGCSE exam in June of Year 5.[1]

Neil Solomon taught that the secret of examinations lay in good preparation. To illustrate his point he produced eight hippos, carved from mubanga wood, of differing weights from a few grams to one of 20 kgs. The biggest hippo portrayed the student who went into the exams unprepared carrying a huge weight around his neck. The well-prepared student was represented by the lightest hippo. Chengelo's first graduates completed their IGCSE exams in June 1991. There was a worry at first because the results went astray, but then in the last week of the August holidays they arrived. There were three candidates, Michael Bentley and Darren Bentley (not related), who had transferred from Sakeji School, and Niamh O'Dowd, who arrived in 1990 from Ireland with her parents on an aid project with the Overseas Development Agency. There was much excitement when the results were announced. Michael got five Cs and a D, Darren got four Bs, two Cs and one E, and Niamh got an A in Mathematics, three Bs, two Cs and one D.

**Progress Reports**
In the early 90s the Board was concerned to know whether the school was on the right lines managerially and academically. In March 1991, Dr Green, on a return visit to the school, made a report to the Board of Governors. He expressed concern over the professional isolation of teaching staff and suggested possible links with

other similar schools, such as Machebeng in Lesotho, Waterford in Swaziland and Maru a Pula in Botswana. He also recommended sabbaticals linked to a course of further study as an inducement to prolong contracts. He wanted roles within the school to be clearly defined, and for properly briefed deputies to be appointed. He advised the Board of Governors not to make decisions and take action that should properly be undertaken by school staff. The Headmaster should generally run the school and look after the academic side. Houseparents should take care of the welfare of pupils, and the Bursar/Administrator should have charge of all administrative staff. He was concerned that, because the Governors had very busy lives, 'the whole burden of academic responsibility plus the social welfare of the children, not to mention the care of the staff, could fall on one pair of shoulders. As the school grows to its intended maximum the Head could easily become an administrator only. I think that this would be a mistake, especially in view of Neil's outstanding ability to teach and relate to children.' Finally Peter Green recommended a UK Support Group. This proposal was to lead in due course to the establishment of the Chengelo Educational Trust with Peter Green himself as Chairman of the Trustees.

Following this second report by Dr Green, the Board began progressively to withdraw from hands-on control and to seek to concentrate on the formulation of policy. However the Governors were cautious about a total withdrawal as they felt that a hands on approach might be needed in certain cultural situations in which the majority of staff were inexperienced. They also took note of Peter Green's comment that the current strategy in the UK for Governors was for the Board to be the inspiration and springboard to the life and ethos of the school.

In June 1992, Michael Chesterman presented his report to the Governors. Michael was at Chengelo in a dual capacity, as acting Headmaster from March to June 1992, and as an educational consultant sponsored by British

Executive Service Overseas. He reported that in his professional judgement Chengelo was on the right lines in both its curriculum policy and in its use of the IGCSE. He found the five heads of department to be competent, as were the subject teachers. Schemes of work were systematically planned and executed. Timetables and exams ran smoothly, with great credit to Ian Richardson. Pupils were motivated and kept busy. But classroom furniture was still incomplete and the sharing of basic course books between parallel sets was a nuisance. Streaming into fast and slow sets according to ability, and the permutation of seven, eight or nine subjects at IGCSE, seemed to work well. The basic seven subjects were English, maths, 2 combined sciences, history or geography, agriculture or French, computers or art or Biblical studies. The extras were English literature, history and geography.

Michael Chesterman made a number of recommendations on the recruitment of local staff, the use of volunteers, the role of the Board and fee levels. The Governors felt that a number of the recommendations were already in hand and not all were practical. It was evident that they felt that they had a parental responsibility to bring the infant school to adulthood, and that at this stage in its life they should not lose control of its development. Overall, Michael's report was upbeat. 'It is a tremendous achievement for non-professionals to have constructed a boarding school in the bush, on a shoestring budget, with simple sketch plans rather than full working drawings, with finance on a hand-to-mouth existence, and tight deadlines to be met non-stop over five years. All this on top of having their own farms to manage.'[2]

## Examination Successes
Ian Richardson's appointment as Headmaster, in January 1996, introduced a number of changes, which have already been mentioned.[3] During Ian Richardson's incumbency

academic results have been consistently high. He inherited a situation where examination results were steadily climbing. Taking five or more passes at Grade C or higher in the IGCSE exams as the benchmark, the percentage of candidates achieving that standard climbed from a low of 25% in 1992, rising to 56% in 1993, and to 90% in 1996. Since then the IGCSE passes at C or above have been consistently well above 80%, ranging from a low of 83% in 2000 to 96% in 2001. In the latest statistics available for 2003, Chengelo students attained a 100% pass rate in grades A*–G (the UK average is 88.6%), and 92% of students gained 5 or more passes at Grade C and above (UK average is 52.6%). 40% of passes were at A* or A grade. The three top students were Chibungo Chisaka (5A*, 3A), Mate Munthali (5A*, 2A,1B) and Twaambo Hamuwele (4A*, 2A, 1B). These are results for which any school anywhere in the world could rightly be proud.

The Chengelo results have been published nationally but comparative results from other schools are not available. Every year the school has to re-register with the Zambian Ministry of Education. This means that the school receives regular inspection from representatives of the Ministry.

**Development Studies**
One of the new subjects was development studies. Roger Allen had introduced the subject at Chengelo before going to Norwich to do a year's MA course in development studies. On his return to Chengelo in 1995 Roger, together with Tim Sims, extended development studies to include a course for Form 3 as well as the IGCSE to Forms 4 and 5. The response from the pupils was enthusiastic.

*I just love babies!' said the fourth form boy, as he beat the previous record by weighing 54 babies in one afternoon! He was participating in a development studies field trip to a local under 5 clinic. The pupils had just discovered that this clinic was helping to save the lives of babies: it had reduced*

ite of malnutrition to 5% compared with 60% in rural
bia as a whole.

ı. is easy to understand why development studies is a vital
part of the Chengelo curriculum. One of the key aims of the
school is to produce future leaders in all areas of Zambia life,
especially the church. The vision is realistic. Out of 70 pupils
doing development studies in the top two years at Chengelo
in 1998, 30 had immediate members of the family who
were either cabinet ministers or members of parliament. In
his speech at the 10th anniversary celebration, David
Moffat urged the pupils to become leaders of integrity and
honesty. Development studies helps pupils to become the
sort of leaders who are not interested in greedy gain, but
have God's heart to serve their country, to protect the poor
(70% or more of Zambians live in absolute poverty) and to
promote justice (Isaiah 58:6-7).

Pupils catch this vision through practical experience
as well as academic study. About 80 pupils are involved
in community service, helping entertain about 120 local
children each week. For a week each year, about 20 pupils
go to Mambilima, a school for physically disabled children
from poor rural villages. Many have testified that their lives
have been changed by their friendships with the Mambilima
pupils. There are several development studies field trips, for
example to local rural development projects and to a local
school and clinic. Pupils also investigate the improvements
at Chengelo, for example the workers' living conditions or
the water scheme (and even the sewage ponds!).

The IGCSE syllabus itself covers a wide range of issues,
which pupils find very relevant to their future lives in
Zambia. They study topics such as: the meaning of
development (this includes historical legacies, such as the
slave trade and colonialism); population; health; education;
rural development; debt and structural adjustment, trade and
aid; gender issues; politics; urbanisation and development
theories (modernisation, dependency and sustainable
development). Pupils are encouraged to express their

*opinions freely in discussions and debates and the standard of debate can be exceptional. They also enjoy videos, role plays and simulation games, such as 'The Farming Game' or 'The Trading Game'. These games are excellent ways of opening up new topics, because the pupils experience the injustices or hardships for themselves and so learn very quickly when we study the issues in detail, using a wide range of booklets and textbooks.*

*As pupils catch God's heart for their country, they also perform outstandingly in the final IGCSE exam (compare Daniel 1:18–20!). 66 pupils have sat the exam in the last two years, 49 have gained an A+ (normally given to the top 2% of pupils internationally) and a further 13 have gained As. 94% of candidates have therefore got A+s or As. Let us give God all the glory and pray that these young people will become the future Daniels of Zambia.*[4]

Now back in England the Allens maintain many friendships with local Zambians formed at Chengelo. Some of them are running churches or church farms that impact large numbers of people in the villages. Roger Allen now works for Christian Aid and finds his memories of Zambia give him a massive motivation when raising HIV awareness or justice issues. Like many who have worked in the Third World, the Allens find it hard to be comfortable back in a Western consumerist society.

## Art Design and Technology

In 1998 the foundations were laid for the new Art Design and Technology Centre. When completed this provided the school with a new art room and pottery centre, a multi-materials workshop, with metal and woodworking equipment, a food and textiles room, and a staff resources room, with a darkroom. The cost of this facility was over £60,000. The building was completed in 1999 but equipping some of the specialist facilities required extra funding. In 2003 13 candidates entered for Art and Design in the IGCSE exam; five received A*s, three As, four Bs, and one a C. As mentioned in Chapter 7, in September 1998 the Neil Solomon Memorial Library was officially dedicated by Ruby (Braumann) Solomon. This provided students with an excellent resource and one of the best collections of books of any school library in Zambia.

## The Sixth Form

In January 2000, after much discussion and debate, the new sixth form opened at Chengelo. Admission to the University of Zambia (UNZA) is on the basis of Ordinary Level or IGCSE exams. But pressure for a sixth form came from parents and pupils, especially from those who wanted to do their undergraduate studies overseas, where Advanced levels were often required for university entrance. Opposition to the expansion to sixth form level came from those who felt that Chengelo would be over-extending its resources. There were also those who feared that Chengelo would be educating its students to work outside of Zambia rather than fulfilling the vision of directly impacting the church and nation within Zambia. Ian Richardson and his deputy, Tim Sims, justified the expansion by arguing that a sixth form would not only further equip the students academically, but would allow a stronger Christian emphasis by the development of a leadership training programme. A new development is the agreement reached with UNZA whereby AS students from Chengelo can be admitted into the University's second year in the engineering and medical faculties.

The construction of the purpose-built primary school allowed its vacated classrooms to be used by the new sixth form. The pioneer sixth form was made up of some twelve boys and girls. The sixth-formers were somewhat apprehensive, but here were some of their early impressions.[5] 'I thought that it would be the same old story all over again: strict routine, living under the constant beady eyes of the staff, annoying day-to-day hassles like the waking up at 6 am, cold showers, and a breakfast that would make even a hardened war veteran's stomach turn. But it was not so. As I unpacked my stuff I thought to myself, "This is something new, I might actually like it."' (Stephen Kashita) 'Before the start of the year I was very apprehensive about A levels at Chengelo. With no purpose-built facilities and a minimum number of teachers I was not convinced by the school's enthusiastic approach. My fears were not well-founded though, as everything has gone to plan and all promises made by Mr Sims have been kept.' (Daniel Richardson)

Students found the academic standards pretty demanding. 'I managed to land myself with a horrible subject combination of maths, physics and chemistry, which, once I got down to it, I thoroughly enjoyed. A levels are a challenge, and at Chengelo an even greater challenge because we are the pioneers. It's new and it's fun and it may even be tough, but we're taking the bull by the horns and going to the top.' (Stephen Kashita) The greater independence of the sixth form was appreciated. 'The atmosphere between staff and pupils is now more relaxed and personal, but the workload has taken a leap, as is expected with A levels. Being pioneers we got pretty excited when new rules and privileges were introduced, like increased independence, responsibility and getting our very own TV and video recorder etc.' (Prity Nathoo) 'The general feeling of independence is highly appreciated by everyone. However we are not exempt from duties, we supervise meals and prep times as the "head" prefects. Most of us do get involved in extra curricular activities, which range from sports to clubs and Christian activities. I am enjoying being part of this establishment!' (Mumba Mumba)

Tembwe Mutungu recognised the central role of Christian leadership training as part of the ethos in the sixth form. 'Amongst the greatest opportunities, in my opinion, has been the opportunity to pursue the International Youth Award at its highest level and the opportunity to put leadership into practice. Even during the first term much fulfilment has been drawn out of leading discipleship groups, working with the youngsters of King's Kids and assisting staff members with duties.'

At the beginning of Term 1 in 2001, the sixth form girls moved into their brand-new hostel, built with a grant of £35,000 from the Beit Trust. Each of its three wings has eight single study-bedrooms, which would be the envy of many universities. The girls were allowed to decorate their rooms to their own design. Each wing has its own spacious bathroom and they share a central common room with the boys. In 2004 the sixth form finally took over the former administration block as a purpose built facility.

The sixth form is now headed by Miss Pauline McKendrick. Chengelo offers a curriculum of AS (Advanced Subsidiary) and A (Advanced) levels through the Cambridge International Examinations (CIE), the same awarding body as the IGCSEs. The subjects offered are art and design, biology, business studies, chemistry, English literature, French, geography, history, maths, physics and religious studies. To be considered for the AS or A level course at Chengelo, students require 5 IGCSE passes at grades A*– C, including English and maths, and at least a B in the subjects selected for AS or A levels.

The level of academic success has steadily improved. In the latest round of examinations in 2003, 75% of all A-level passes were grades A–C, and 68% of all AS-Level passes were A–D. Top students were Mumba Mumba (A,A,B at A-level, A at AS-level), Kevin Street (A,A,B at A-level), Laura Street (A,A,C at A-level), Lukundo Namusamba (A,B,C at A-level), Hansjorg Shultheiss (A,A,A,B at AS-level).

## Music

Music has not been forgotten at Chengelo. On 4th July 1991, eight Chengelo students, all girls, travelled down to Lusaka for their piano exams. Esther Kamata described the exam. 'The students were tested on a cool Thursday morning at Evelyn Hone College. All of them were well-prepared but also nervous because for most, it was their first exam. The invigilator was from the Royal School of Music in London and what would be called "a typical Englishman", (tiny glasses on the tip of his nose, grey hair and sideburns). This sight amazed the girls, but they still managed to come out of the exam room in one piece very much relieved it was all over.... During the August holidays, the marks arrived – all the hard work was rewarded with good marks – four distinctions, three merits and one pass. A very worthwhile effort and thanks to Miss van Gend for all her hard work.'[6] Over the years a number of staff have looked after music at Chengelo. In 1997 a cassette of 'Chengelo Songs' was produced. This featured Mrs Carla van der Maas as lead vocalist with backing vocals from the school choir accompanied by Mr Keesjan van der Maas.

Currently, Miss Delwyn Houghton from New Zealand, is Head of Music. Delwyn has continued the individual piano tuition formerly led by Miss Claire Matthews and Miss Amy Bishop, and she has introduced regular evening piano concerts, which have become one of the highlights of the school calendar. In the primary school each class has a regular weekly music lesson, and many pupils are learning recorder under the tuition of Miss Hannah Flanders. Mike Hackston contributed significantly to the development of worship music and the training of the choir for the Sunday evening celebration. There are now primary and secondary choirs, and a worship band with keyboard, electric guitar, bass and drums, which regularly plays on Sunday evenings at the Fusion celebration.

## Art

Art itself has always been a strong feature at Chengelo. When the school first opened there was inevitably a shortage of good quality paper, paint and brushes. But Mr David Rust and other teachers improvised and gradually the necessary equipment arrrived. One of David Rust's major achievements was to organise the painting of the mural on the east wing of the dining hall. Initially Mr Rust got the Form 3s and 4s to paint animals in bright colours to express the way that bright colours can bring out feelings. This resulted in pink leopards and green giraffes. This led to the idea of an eye-catching mural. The art class photocopied the chosen pictures and then drew grids on the walls to scale-up the pictures. After the drawings were all up on the wall, the painting started, using emulsion paint. There was a pillar in the middle of the mural with a lion on each side facing away from each other. Below one of the lions was a tree-frog and below the other lion a snake. Going outwards from the snake was a crocodile and then a beautiful sun silhouette. On the other side was a buffalo, an underwater scene and a swan. When each individual had done their bit, the task of blending the pictures so that the colours flowed into one another was entrusted to David Domingo, Talja Parkinson and George Nicoll. After one-and-a- half terms the mural was completed on the afternoon of the last day, just in time for prize giving.[7]

In March 1998 Chengelo played host to the fourth Arts Festival of the Independent Schools Association of Zambia. Over two hundred students and staff were present from nine visiting schools, and over the weekend a wide variety of dance, drama and music was performed, together with an accompanying exhibition of artwork. The continued high standard of Chengelo art is reflected in the good IGCSE results (e.g. 5 A*s out of 13 candidates in Art and Design in 2001). At the Chengelo Fellowship Day at Martlesham Heath in East Anglia on 5th April 2003, visitors were able to see an excellent sample of art work from the school, exhibited on the walls. This exhibition was organised by Mr Saul Tembo, Chengelo's accomplished art teacher. As mentioned earlier, Saul spent five weeks as artist-in-residence at Katharine Lady Berkeley's School in Gloucestershire in the early part of 2003, and worked with groups of pupils to produce an outdoor mural with an African theme for the main area of the school. As well as his artwork, Saul spent time with English pupils talking about African culture and sharing his Christian faith.

## Shows, Plays and Musicals

From its inception Chengelo has established a tradition of putting on shows, plays and musicals.[8] *From Pharoah to Freedom* was the first full-scale musical tackled by the school. One-and-a-half hours of fairly continuous singing, broken only by narrative passages, read expressively by Mpande Simumba, told the story of Israel's escape from bondage to freedom. Mr Rust and Mr Chambwe (cattle manager for David Moffat) took the leading roles of Aaron and Moses, and Annette Cowham sang some beautiful solos. The musical was staged in the dining-hall with a backdrop of an Egyptian mural. The Egyptian theme was followed by *Joseph and His Amazing Technicolour Dreamcoat*, staged in May 1991, and produced by Mrs Solomon, Miss van Gend and Mr Cudmore. Simon Robinson played the part of Joseph with Andrew Domingo as Jacob and Ian Richardson at Potiphar. Fred Katongo as Pharoah delighted the audience with his 'Elvis' scene. *Joseph* had a number of performances including one for the Mkushi farmers and one for parents on Open Day. Other early productions included a *Round-the-World Christmas*, memorable for Mweshi Ng'andwe cycling across the stage as a Dutch girl in skirt and blouse and blond pigtails, and *Fawlty Towers*, produced by Mr Rust in Term 3, 1991. Sacha Fertig played Basil and Amy Cantlay played Sybil. Despite David Rust saying that the production was best forgotten, the show's humour and its technical mishaps kept the audience in fits of laughter.

Recently, the school has attempted some fairly ambitious productions. In July 2000 four performances were given of the musical *My Fair Lady*,[9] produced by Lawrence Richardson with assistance from Hannah Flanders and Claire Matthews. Charity Namfukwe rose to the challenge of playing Eliza Doolittle and getting her tongue around the Cockney vowels of the young flower-girl and then the high-falutin' accents and mannerisms of the society beauty. The transformation of this young lady was effected by Professor Higgins, well played by Tembwe Mutungu in an inimitable and convincing fashion. Tony Siddle enjoyed himself as Eliza's father, singing his 'Get me to the church on time' with gusto. Lin Carter created some great props and costumes.

Chengelo had gone on tour back in 1996, when a production of Shakespeare's *Twelfth Night* was taken to Mkushi, Kitwe and Lusaka. In 2002 it was Shakespeare's *A Midsummer Night's Dream*[10] which occupied a cast of 25 actors for a gruelling routine of fifteen weeks of rehearsals, often three times a week. Trevor Roff, the director, expected the highest standards. 'He was a perfectionist,' moaned one actor. It was 'frustration, fatigue, laughter and tears', according to Charity Namfukwe, who played Titania. But the actors learnt that despite the hard work they could enjoy themselves and, 'the atmosphere was full of humour and friendship from the first rehearsal'. 'I discovered a mischievous part of myself in playing Puck,' said Ntiusya Mutala. Melanie Patching found, 'I could really become the part of Hermia,' and Chibungo Chisaka, who played Bottom, realised that, 'to make people laugh is a blessing and a gift'. Four performances took place before some 700 people. The first two were in Ndola and Lusaka, where one audience member reported that the second half was the funniest performance ever seen in the Playhouse. Returning to Chengelo's Grandstand, the first performance was bedevilled with sickness. But all came together for the final performance. 'I was sick with laughter', said one staff member. And Laura Kapolyo, who played Helena, summed it all up when she said, 'It was an overwhelming feeling as we watched the audience dissolve into fits of laughter.' The latest Shakespearean play to be directed by Trevor Roff is *The Merchant of Venice*.

## An Educationalist's Assessment

Let us give the last word to Dr. Peter Green for his assessment of Chengelo as a school. 'Chengelo has developed. I was last there in 2002. That confirmed that Chengelo is a very good educational establishment, a very good school indeed. By very good, I mean educationally, socially and in terms of educational development. Of course there are things which could be improved. I have worked in sixteen African countries and on the basis of comparison with other schools, Chengelo certainly rates among the top. I think that it is invidious to compare with schools in the UK because a school serves a culture. Chengelo serves Zambian culture. I think Chengelo is an excellent school for Zambia and I just hope that it remains so.'[11]

## Notes

[1] Chengelo's school year originally started in September and then was changed to January in 1989 to fit in with the Zambian education system.

[2] Report on Chengelo School by Michael Chesterman, presented to the Board of Governors, 27 June 1992.

[3] See Chapter 5.

[4] Article by Roger Allen, Head of Development Studies, *Chengelo Educational Trust Newsletter*, No. 9, March 1999.

[5] *Chengelo Educational Trust Newsletter*, No. 12, July 2000.

[6] *Chengelo: The First Three Years*, p. 68.

[7] Op cit., pp. 67-68, article by George Nicoll.

[8] Op cit., pp. 66-67, see article by Andreas Nebel and others.

[9] See Review in *Chengelo Educational Trust Newsletter*, No. 13, December 2000.

[10] See *Chengelo Educational Trust Newsletter*, No. 17, December 2002.

[11] Interview with author, 24.04.04.

# Chapter Ten

# The Body

## The Creation of the Sports Field

'*Mens sana in sano corpore*', a sound mind in a healthy body, has always been a guiding principle in Chengelo's philosophy. Of course, the school started with nothing. It was Barton Young who made himself responsible for the sports fields and the campus gardens. He gave of his time and his men and machines to turn what was a rough piece of bush into something resembling a level playing field. Barton joked that in those days his wife questioned whether he was married to her or to Chengelo. As we have seen, David Rust played a leading role in marking out some of the earliest areas for games. By the start of the first term he had worked with a gang of labourers and levelled and marked out two badminton courts, two volleyball courts, and a netball court. The table tennis table consisted of two dining room tables put end to end. In addition there was space for rounders and football. Under the influence of Neil Solomon there was a strong emphasis on cross-country running, so staff and pupils kept pretty fit.

The early pioneers will never forget the day when they were called upon by Mr Solomon to plant the whole playing field with grass. When they visit the school today and look out at the splendid greensward they can feel justly proud that their efforts that muddy day helped to create the magnificent turf today. The arrival of Sylvia Chesterman, a professional sports coach, at Chengelo was the next step. Together with Barton Young and a team of workers, Sylvia measured and laid out most of the existing sports facilities.

'Sylvia has found plenty of scope and is not just "tagging along". To take advantage of her specialist coaching skills, netball practice has been declared compulsory – by the girls, not by us. Out there in the field beyond the water-furrow she is pegging out an athletics track, strategically sited between the anthills. In addition to the athletics track Sylvia has pegged out a whole sports complex comprising 3 basketball courts, 2 soccer pitches, a rugby field, 3 netball courts and 4 volleyball courts.... This has involved many hours of careful measuring out in the sun (under a straw hat), and supervision of labourers slashing grass and levelling out humps and bumps. Two tractors with mud scoops, grass-cutting blades and hay-rakes have added power and pace to the process. Sideline incidents include the smoking out of snakes from anthills!'[1]

## The Swimming Pool

The first swimming pool was a 10m x 4m pool next to the old farmhouse of Lilanda. David Rust managed to get it operational. It was quite muddy as the water came from the furrow and there was no filter. Desmond Hitchins describes the swimming training in the early days. 'Charles Krogh was the team captain. He had a lot of experience in training, so he was asked by the coach to help train the others. He had the whole team going around the tiny pool propelling themselves with their legs only, treading water for ten minutes with their arms in the air, and twenty length warm-down at the end. Diving practice was one thing he never gave up on. The swimmers would be in and out of the pool till they got it perfect.... In 1991 when the new school pool still was not completed, the team had to use the Moffats' pool for training. They usually ran there (about one and a half kilometres). At the pool they would either swim six lengths, only three swimmers at a time, or swim five times around the pool in convoy, for warming up.'[2]

The school pool was placed by the sports field, alongside the proposed squash and tennis courts. During August 1991, Barton Young used his tractors with dam scoops to dig out the pool site, which was then shaped by the workmen. After the floor and sides were sealed, the tiles were laid in the pool. When it was completed it was filled with water from the furrow, and then purified with the addition of lime, chlorine and salt. The pool is 25 metres long with seven lanes and a constant depth of 1.5 metres. Amidst great excitement, the pool was officially opened by Barton Young on 17th November 1991.

Mpande Simumba described the scene. 'The colourfully dressed pupils lined up along three sides of the pool and at a given signal by Mr Solomon, they all stepped forward holding hands on to the slate tiles. Mr Young then pushed Margaret Nicoll into the pool; she in turn pulled the next person in and so on... until all 150 pupils were in the water. When the last person fell in, the whole school submerged under the water for five seconds. When they surfaced, they sang "For he's a jolly good fellow". After the song, there was total commotion, as everyone splashed, shouted and swam all over the pool. Laughter and shrieks rang through the air as Mr Solomon and Mr Young flung themselves into the water fully dressed. Not surprisingly Mr Solomon forgot to take off his shoes.'[3]

With the arrival of the new pool, swimming lessons were organised for beginners. It became school policy that everyone should learn to swim before they left in Form 5.

Chengelo had become a member of the Zambia Amateur Swimming Union, and with Miss Lisa Davenport and Miss Sue Steele-Smith as enthusiastic coaches, standards in swimming showed a steady improvement. School galas were organised between the two school houses, Chisela and Bulaya, and Chengelo started to compete against other schools. In October 1991 the school competed in their third competition at Simba School in Ndola. The two girls swimming in the 13/14 year olds individual medley thought that they had come first and second, until they were told that they were disqualified for doing only one length of each stroke instead of two. Despite this disappointment, Chengelo swimmers acquitted themselves with credit, showed good sportsmanship and returned to school with their heads high. In December 1993 the school discovered that five of its swimmers, Stephanie Smith, Allan Greig, Charles Krogh, Zanetta Nyendwa and Jerome Krogh, all held national records for their age groups.

Michael Chesterman reported in his Bush Telegraph in March 1992, 'At midday today we heard tremendous shouts and cheers from the dining-hall. No, not a food riot but the lorry returning with our swimming team and the inter-secondary schools Challenge Cup —a trophy dominated for the last 20 years by the International School in Lusaka. What an encouragement and morale-booster!'

**Soccer**
Soccer naturally featured as one of Chengelo's favourite sports, certainly for the boys. The first coaches were Mr Tresford Mukuka, the Moffats' crops manager, and Mr Evan Mbozi, teacher of French and English. At first the school had no pitch, so the players had to jog the one kilometre or so to the Moffats' pitch. The next pitch was by the school entrance gates. This also meant a good jog before the games, but it kept the players fit. The very first match was against the Moffats' workers, who were the clear favourites. The school lost 2-3, which was a good result,

but was bettered in the second match which was a draw at 3-3. Chengelo's first match against Nkolonga Primary school resulted in a humiliating defeat 6-0, but this was more than avenged in the return match with a win for the school, 10-1. This winning streak was maintained against another local school, Chalata Secondary. The result was a 6-3 triumph for Chengelo. In June 1991, Chengelo, the under-dogs, defeated Simba School, Ndola 5-2.

Roger Allen remembers early days with the football team. 'I remember playing in one match where the opposition did not have boots, and one of the opposition actually burst the ball because his toes nails were so long. This was out in one of the local schools. The Chengelo boys would generally have boots but would take them off if the opposition did not have them. I remember that you would get up at 5 am and pile into one of David Moffat's farm lorries with a load of mattresses and everybody on top. A five-hour journey up to Ndola and we would arrive about 10. When we arrived some of the boys were very dizzy from imbibing the fumes on the way. After a triangular tournament we would pile back into the lorry for the five-hour journey back to the school.'[4]

## Rugby and Other Sports
Rugby was popular in the early days at Chengelo. Mike Robinson was the first rugby coach. The first match was against the International School in Lusaka. On the day before the match, twenty enthusiastic boys climbed into a lorry packed with mattresses. Arriving in Lusaka, the team were fed by Mrs Nduna and Mrs Schulz. The next day, at Lusaka showgrounds, Chengelo showed their mettle and defeated the International School after a hard physical game by 40 points to 11. Not to be confused with rugby was 'rugger', a game invented by two visiting doctors, Dr Levers and Dr Watters. This was a form of touch rugby played by two teams of ten members each and with no running allowed. Another game, introduced

by Mr Richardson, was 'stone age football', which was a kind of Eton wall game played in the mud with a football and two teams of any number a side. Mr Solomon also introduced the school to flingelo, a game between two teams, with a frisbee instead of a ball.

The girls began competitive netball with a series of impressive wins over the local secondary school, Chalata. When Simba School visited from Ndola, Chengelo scored a decisive win of 19-9. The girls encountered their first thrashing when they went to play Mpelembe School in Kitwe and were beaten 21-4 in the first game, and 6-3 in the second. During Term 2 in 1991, the boys and girls at Chengelo tried to escape from the usual sexual stereotypes. The girls played football, but often found themselves being blown up by the referee for handball. The boys played netball in skirts, and their antics certainly brought much entertainment to the spectating girls.

Running was an important part of the school regime. Every Saturday there was a compulsory time trial on a marked course. Starting at the old farmhouse, the route went along the back road past the compound and straight along to the gum-trees that meet the Kingdoms' road. Then it turned right and went up to the site of the present entrance gates and then back to the school. This distance of exactly four kilometres took about 30 minutes on average. The first athletics sports consisted of 100 metres sprints, 400 metres and 800 metres relays and a walking race. Bulaya narrowly beat Chisela 100-97. In the course of time the 18 kms Rock Ridge run from the Youngs' farm to the school became an important fixture on the school calendar.

From those early days, sport at Chengelo has made impressive progress. In 1995 the arrival of Tim Foster, an ex-Sakeji boy, brought the school a sports specialist and a fine PE teacher. As a result of his input and Mrs Louise Thomas' hard work with the swimming team, Chengelo reached new heights when eight of its swimmers were selected to represent Zambia in an international gala in Lusaka. On the journey down, the whole team suffered a near fatal accident when their minibus left the road, overturned and plunged into a ditch. Miraculously nobody was injured. Amazingly the swimmers went on to compete in the gala, and brought back one silver, and four bronze, medals. About this time the grandstand was completed at the pool and two tennis courts were ready for commissioning. A squash court with a fine tooth and tongue flooring was built by Don Stacey, a local farmer, and replaced the converted barn loaned by Barton Young.

In 1996 Chengelo won the korfball competition in the African Championships held in Pretoria. Not many people may have heard of korfball, but it is a game similar to netball and basketball, invented in the Netherlands. It was a Dutchman, Mr van der Maas, who introduced Chengelo to the game, and the school took to the game so well that it was rewarded with international success in this niche sport.

**Sporting Triumphs**

The year 2000 was one of all round sports success when the senior and junior girls' netball teams were winners at the Independent Schools Sports Festival. The boys were not to be outdone with both senior and junior soccer teams winning their tournaments. Also in 2000, ten of Chengelo's swimmers represented Zambia in an international competition against Kenya. The following year Chengelo's 1st XI football team won the Independent Schools Association of Zambia (ISAZ) trophy, and retained the trophy in 2002 when they beat Ibex Hill in the final, the result being decided by a 'golden goal'. Sadly, the girls' basketball team lost to the International School 5-4. Apart from football success, the senior rugby team enjoyed a two-year unbeaten run against other school teams, and the girls' netball team were unbeaten for four years. In

2003 Chengelo took four out of the six trophies available at the ISAZ Festival, and Gemma Campbell was named 'Sportsperson of the Tournament'.

Chengelo has its Head of Physical Education, Steve Bannister, who, with his wife, Veronica, arrived at Chengelo in September 2000. If asked why Chengelo teams are so successful, Steve will say that it is due to the skill and enthusiasm of the pupils together with the excellent foundation laid by his predecessors, Tim Foster, Megan Richardson, and Jon and Sarah Stamford. It was Jon Stamford who obtained special seed to lay out a cricket square, which he carefully tended and rolled until he had produced a beautiful green. However there can be little doubt that credit for recent successes must go to Steve and his present staff team for their total commitment and dedication to excellence. Steve Bannister points to the value of team sports in encouraging co-operative effort and good personal relationships. It was very creditable that during Term 1 in 2003 it was reported that 65% of the boys and 45% of the girls represented Chengelo in one or more competitive sports fixtures. Most of those participated in the team sports of basketball, football, netball and rugby. At the end of 2004 Steve led the school basketball team on a tour in England with matches in Northampton, Woodbridge, Wellingborough and Peterborough, culminating in a reception at the Zambian High Commission.

Horse-riding is one of Chengelo's attractions. It was Barton Young who built the six smart stables and the tack room at the bottom end of the school. First riding lessons took place at the Moffats' farm on their gelding, 'Bracken', which, sadly, had to be put down. The first three horses acquired by the school, two geldings and a stallion, moved in once the water supply was installed. They have been followed by other horses. Mrs Di Parker-Dennison has been involved with horseriding from the start, combining this with her work as librarian. Her total commitment to the stables and her professional riding lessons have made a big impact.

## The Great Outdoors

The great outdoors was one of Neil Solomon's consuming passions. Neil took the boys camping in all weathers, and probably they remembered the rainy camps best of all.[5] He would take the children walking on long moonlit walks. He encouraged pupils to learn the basics of bushcraft, such as making shelters in bad weather, and how to construct ovens out of anthills for cooking and baking. Orienteering taught fast thinking, code breaking and map reading, as well as physical fitness. Favourite places for visits were the Youngs' farm and the Kingdoms' dam. The walk to Rock Ridge, the Youngs' farm, was a strenuous one of some 18 kms, but the pupils were rewarded on arrival with Yvonne Young's famed hospitality, with lots of food and squash to drink, as well as the waterslide, volleyball and other games. The Kingdoms' dam was about 45 minutes walk from the school. Canoeing and swimming were popular in the dam, until crocodile prints were seen in the vicinity. The Mkushi River was nearer, only about 20 minutes walk, and pupils enjoyed fishing or just relaxing there. Bonfires were always popular at Chengelo, and the saving of England's Parliament from Guy Fawkes was celebrated with great enthusiasm in the African bush some four hundred years later. As November 5th was a day before the Hindu festival of 'Diwali', the fireworks were kindly provided in the early days by the Patel family.

Neil Solomon was a great believer in the character-building qualities of 'the platform'. The first pupils to be introduced to the platform were a group of eight girls. The platform was made of wooden poles and measured 1.5m x 1.5m. It was some two metres off the ground and consisted of two levels. A lower floor served as storage space for pots and provisions. A hole in the corner acted as a latrine. The higher platform had to house the eight girls and a fire for cooking. The rules of the platform were simple: the girls were not allowed down on the ground for 24 hours, and had to keep very quiet so that they could not be heard by Mr Solomon in his house, some 10 metres away. Zeles Zulu who was a member of the first group describes how at one stage the girls found it difficult to all sit down. They became impatient and started screaming at each other. 'Sleeping was very uncomfortable. In the middle of the night some woke up and started complaining. So we had to rearrange the sleeping bags and put them in a better position.... We had to take it in turns to sleep lying down, four at a time, while the other four sat up.... The next day all the girls seemed comfortable and happy, though we were starving by now.... We stayed on the platform longer than twenty-four hours because Mr Solomon forgot about us.'[6]

The platform came to a sudden end when a group of Form 1 boys camped there in their first term in 1990 Regrettably, one of the boys stoked the fire so big that it set light to a sleeping bag. In the panic that ensued, the boys jumped off the platform and the whole structure caught fire. The platform was replaced by a two-roomed hut on the banks of the Mkushi river. The hut was constructed by six Form 3 boys over the Heroes and Unity weekend. They began in high spirits but, as the weekend wore on, they began to flag. Bupe Pihlblad wrote: 'The work continued day after day, blisters appeared everywhere.... We were all fed up with camping, all our clothes were dirty, we were running short of food, and we were tired.'[7] They were all so exhausted that they never heard that they had an intruder. Andrew Moffat decided to spend the night at the campsite, and despite dancing and singing, he could not wake them from their sleep. But his arrival brought some solace. Andrew ran home and got his Land Rover so that the whole party could have a lift back to school. The boys were treated as heroes and their unity was restored.

An exercise brought from Treverton by Neil Solomon

was called 'Solitaire'. It was essentially an exercise in meditating or contemplating. The idea is to sit pupils at such a distance from one another so that they cannot talk. Each pupil is allowed only a Bible, pen and paper. The idea is to explore one's own inmost thoughts. Chengelo pupils found this hard at first, but gradually warmed to the whole process. The first meditation exercise was introduced in 1989 when a group of about 20 pupils went camping in the Chilongoma Hills. Later, some pupils tried 'solitairing' for a whole 24 hours, but Neil Solomon himself advocated that really to benefit from the exercise it should take place over 72 hours.

In July 1991 the first Chengelo ascent of Mount Mpumpu was attempted. The party was led by Mr Rust, and consisted of seven Form 4 boys, three Form 2 boys, Mr and Mrs George and the Rea family. Base camp was established at Changwena, near a waterfall and three rock pools. Leaving three of the party at base camp, the climbers at first light made their way up the mountain. To reach the summit of Mount Mpumpu at 6,300 feet they had to enter a large, bat-infested cave with an unbearable stench. Then they had to pass through a narrow tunnel. After a hard walk across jagged rocks, the summit was reached at 14.30. A campsite was then found and the party slept under the stars. The following day, the climbers made their way to Fort Elwes, built in the early colonial period. They reached base camp that evening, tired and weary but satisfied. They had discovered for themselves that Zambia is not all flat savannah country.

It was Tim Cripps who constructed the 'ropes course' at the main school in 1993. This became very popular with boys and girls who learnt to overcome their fear of heights and their own limitations as they climbed and swung high above the ground.

## Ndubaluba

There are two memorials to Neil Solomon at Chengelo. One is the Neil Solomon Library, which reflects Neil's love of books and learning. The other, which does not bear his name but is undoubtedly his special baby, is Ndubaluba. 'Ndubaluba' means Lady Ross' Laurie. It is a beautiful bird, which makes a very high-pitched cry, 'dbu dbu'. Neil Solomon believed that pupils could learn more from five days spent in the wild than from five weeks in a classroom. When he retired as Headmaster of Chengelo in 1993, after five years' pioneering work, Neil moved to Ndubaluba to pursue a career in writing and research. He also envisaged Ndubaluba as a Centre for correspondence A-level courses at a time when there were few facilities in Zambia for pursuing advanced level studies. Neil and his family all moved to Ndubaluba where they lived simply in a very basic house. The December 1993 Parents' Newletter was written by Neil at his outdoor desk at Ndubaluba, with a computer and printer using a 12 volt solar-charged battery.

The school had used Ndubaluba at various times in the early days. Ndubaluba stands 14 kilometres distance from Chengelo. Formerly, it was farmed by Pelle Johansson. In Term 3 of 1991, the whole Form 1 class of 55 pupils spent a week at Ndubaluba. The different lessons each day were all related to the farm. Mr Ngulube got his maths class to measure the area of Mr Johansson's maize field near the camp. Mrs Solomon's geography class did a survey of the workers' compound to find out how many people lived there and what were the schooling facilities. For history, Mr Rust got an old farm worker to describe earlier farmers and the work on the farm. In the afternoons the class learnt how to make bread, how to pound maize, how to pluck a chicken, and how to make charcoal.

Eventually, Neil Solomon's deteriorating health meant that he had to leave Ndubaluba and return with his family to South Africa. Richard Thompson had come out to

Chengelo to teach geography, and from Neil learnt how his heart was for Ndubaluba to be an outdoor Centre. The land actually belonged to the Moffat family but they agreed that the site could be developed for an outdoor Centre. Richard Thompson agreed to go and live at Ndubaluba to get the Centre going.

Ndubaluba adopted the following vision statement: 'With the unique interaction of outdoor pursuits, environment, expressive arts and community development projects, Ndubaluba provides opportunities for personal growth, sensitive interaction with the natural surroundings and its people, ultimately drawing them closer to God. This experience aims to facilitate long-term positive change within Zambia and beyond.' The Christian ethos of the Centre is foundational to the vision. The theology of Ndubaluba stresses God as Creator of the natural world and of all humanity. People have a responsibility to care for the earth and to enter into a relationship with the Creator.

Richard Thompson is now the Head of Outdoor Education and the Ndubaluba Centre. He made the crossover from classroom teaching to outdoor education by doing fieldwork and training with the Abernethy Trust in Scotland. There he picked up qualifications in mountaineering, rock climbing, canoeing, orienteering and first aid. Richard looks like a very fit and healthy young man. But his appearance today belies the fact that only two years earlier, when climbing in the Ruwenzori Mountains in Uganda, he became ill with altitude sickness and was rushed to hospital with cerebral malaria and pulmonary pneumonia. Happily, Richard made a good recovery. As Richard led members of the CET party around the site in May 2004, he described how Ndubaluba had developed.[8]

*In the first few years it just took Chengelo students. Slowly we have expanded and seen the need in the country for an outdoor Centre. Gradually, more schools have started*

189

*coming and it has got bigger and bigger. It is seen as a good thing. Right now we have five staff and we are running courses right through the year. The staff includes Alex (Britton), Colin (McMaster), and we are just getting a Zambian trainee staff member in a month's time. It is quite difficult to get trained Zambians. There is an outward bound Centre at Mbala, but it has not been very operational so Ndubaluba is quite special in Zambia. So we are getting a lady to come and will do a training course for her. We are looking to get more Zambians on the instructional staff. We have also got Priscilla (Mambwe) our cook. And then James (Chipapala) is our supervisor and does some instructing. We have got about three or four guys who look after the site and do the security.*

*The buildings have developed over time. We have a girls' side and a boys' side and this is the dining-room and the kitchen. We have different activities around here. I have my house here. Colin and Chênelle (McMaster) live over there.*

*We have got some money from the Beit Trust. The next project is another staff house. We will have an equipment store and a small reception area where groups come on arrival. Then we are going to have an environmental classroom.*

*The sort of activities that we do are very much like the outward bound courses: rock climbing, canoeing, walking, hiking. We do the International Youth Award, the equivalent of the Duke of Edinburgh's. This is very popular here.*

*When I first came, I remember looking at a photo of a group who had been on a trip. It was quite noticeable that a lot of the students were white or coloured (mixed-race). The IYA has been quite good in bridging that gap and getting a lot of Zambian students interested in outdoor education. A lot of the students and their parents would see the bush as a step backwards. They have just come to the city. But the certificate is valued at university, and as character development, and a lot more Zambians are now interested. And as the school has developed, outdoor education is much more established.*

*We have a compulsory aspect whereby every student will do one week of outdoor education each year. This runs right through secondary schooling. We have an internal award called the Rumdoodle Award,[9] and the IYA (International Youth Award). They are optional and voluntary.*

*We are employed by the school and have the same conditions. We usually work through the holidays. We do expressive arts and community projects in the villages, such as building, especially with UK groups. We get an organisation here called World Challenge, and we go up on Mount Mpumpu. It is about 6,300 feet —higher than Ben Nevis.*

*The aim of the Centre is all to do with character development and spiritual growth. We see the Chengelo students each year and we can build on that. We have an evangelistic outreach to all the groups that come here. We hopefully challenge them as appropriate with the gospel. Out here with the activities they are a bit more open to talk —get them a bit closer to God.*

*I keep in touch with a lot of ex-students and a lot of the value comes after they have left. They say, 'I learnt so much from this and I miss this or that.' One boy came back, a guy called Kupa Mutungu, and he has got into Princeton University in the United States and he said he had to write four essays, and three of them were on the outdoor aspect of education of Chengelo. 'These were the things that I really learnt about life and about myself.'*

*They can start the IYA in Form 3 when they are 14. This year we have about 90% doing bronze, and I am not sure whether all will be going on to silver, perhaps 24 out of 50. Then the sixth form is coming tomorrow, and that is 8 students out of 16 —about 50%. We do the final on Lake Tanganyika. It can be difficult in the sixth form because of the pressure of academic work. Last year we had four doing gold, but none got the Award although they are*

191

*continuing. This year we have five and we hope that three of them will get the Award. And we are hoping that President Mwanawasa, the President of the Award in Zambia, will give out the gold Awards. There are only two schools doing gold. Others are doing bronze and silver.*

*We are included in the school accounts. We broke even two years ago. Last year we made a small profit.*

*We need a long wheel based Landrover costing £15,000. We've raised £3,000.*

Participants for the silver International Youth Award must complete two expeditions, a 'practice' and a 'qualifying' venture. Both trips must incorporate the following: three nights out, two nights in a shelter or tent, 21 hours of effort (averaging seven hours a day) and a hike totalling 48 km. Participants walk in groups of between three and seven. They must carry food for three days, water, stove, pots and pans, tents and sleeping bags. Sibongwile Namfukwe wrote a diary of her expedition to the Chipota Falls. 'The Silver Expedition was the most amazing experience of my life because of all the wonderful and beautiful things I saw in nature and because of the deeper trust and love I found in God.... We managed to persevere when our hearts lacked motivation, and we managed to endure beyond our pains (and blisters!) and anxieties, not giving up but going on, because we knew God was with us and we could feel him taking care of us; even in that dambo, where we thought we would drown, he rescued us.'[10]

The value of the Ndubaluba courses is increasingly appreciated by students and employers alike. The Centre is now being used by a variety of outside groups such as local school groups, the farm school teachers, Christians in Action, and Boys and Girls Brigade groups. On a recent leadership course these remarks were made by two young Zambians: 'Despite the problems there are ways round them for solutions' (Anderson); 'We have been taught to think wide, not the way we have been' (Edith). Pupils from

Mambilima, the special school for children with physical disabilities, have attended Ndubaluba for courses. The Deputy Head noted in a letter after a course: 'I know my pupils will never be the same again as they have learnt to have self-confidence, trust their friends and offer help to those who cannot perform certain tasks.'[11]

In Term 2 of 1998, all of Form 4s took part in an intensive leadership training course at Ndubaluba. They heard seminars on counselling skills, leadership styles, public speaking and servant leadership, as well as doing some initiative exercises and playing a strenuous wide game, called 'Capture the Flag'. The Form 4s later put their training into action. Working in small groups, they organised and executed a health education seminar for local workers, an evangelistic event at a nearby village, a formal dinner for Forms 3 and 4, a picnic for the primary children and other activities.

One anonymous quotation displayed at Ndubaluba reads: 'A good leader is one whose followers have confidence in the leader. A great leader is one whose followers have confidence in themselves.' Richard Thompson has written: 'Outdoor education and leadership courses develop and test qualities essential to good leadership. Courage to try something new, perseverance never to give up, integrity to stand firm, compassion to put others first, co-operation to support them, creativity to think widely, initiative to allow ideas to become action and an overriding spiritual strength to give purpose.'[12]

## Conclusion

Bob Baker, as an experienced former secondary headteacher in the English state system, is in good position to sum up Chengelo's sporting facilities. 'The sports facilities in general would be very good compared to the UK. The squash courts and swimming pool are particularly good.' He considers that the facilities would stand up well against some of the better independent schools in Britain. Furthermore, 'Chengelo has an excellent environment in which sports can be developed – the Kingdom dam for watersports – the outward bound type "assault course" – the facilities at the Ndubaluba outdoor education Centre – but the question is whether or not these have been fully developed. It must be remembered that Chengelo has the great advantage of almost unlimited space.' Finally, Bob Baker would like to see more attention given to the promotion of indoor games such as table tennis and snooker.[13]

**Notes**

[1] Michael and Sylvia Chesterman's *Bush Telegraph*, March 1992.

[2] *Chengelo: The First Three Years*, p 79.

[3] Ibid., p. 80.

[4] Interview with the author 19.03.04.

[5] See the story of one rainy camp in Chapter 4.

[6] Ibid., p. 86.

[7] Ibid., p. 88.

[8] Conversation taped by author at Ndubaluba 18.05.04. See also web site: www.ndubaluba.com

[9] The award is a demanding test of the Chengelo students' bravery, determination and outdoor competence. It involves mountain climbing, rafting, diving, rock climbing, swinging, running, and sleeping at the top of a 70 ft tree. Very few achieve the levels necessary to gain the award each year, but to the few who do it is Chengelo's ultimate challenge.

[10] Article in Parents' *Newsletter*, No 4, July 1998. Article by Richard Thompson in *Horizons* (23), Autumn 2003, the magazine of the Institute for Outdoor Learning.

[11] Ibid.

[12] Note to the author sent as email attachment dated 07.02.05.

# Chapter Eleven

# The Spirit

## The Christian Ethos

Chengelo was founded as a specifically Christian school. But what is a Christian school? To pose the question is to invite a whole spectrum of views as to what constitutes a school as a Christian one. From the first, the founders of Chengelo determined that the school should find a middle way between offering just a veneer of Christianity and being a spiritual hothouse. This middle way should provide high academic standards and give opportunity for young people to develop their full God-given abilities in all spheres by including a range of practical and outdoor activities in addition to classroom learning. The school should aim to give pupils a positive exposure to Christianity and to equip pupils for life in modern society.

The Christian ethos at Chengelo is based on five principles:[1]

- God is acknowledged and taught as the Creator and Sustainer of all things.
- Knowledge of the Triune God is considered essential for balanced physical, mental and social development.
- Each individual person is seen as having a specific value in the eyes of God, and therefore all types

of gifts, abilities and personalities are given equal opportunity.
- Biblical moral standards are taught as unchanging.
- All teaching and administrative staff are committed Christians.

The overall aim was that Chengelo should be a lighthouse of educational merit and Christian virtue. When the Governors reviewed the Christian ethos of Chengelo, in October 1995, it was noted that there were fewer practising Christians attending the school than when it started, there were more parents in financial difficulties and there were more boys and girls from difficult backgrounds. There was concern expressed that Zambia would move towards secular humanism despite the fact that President Chiluba had declared Zambia a Christian country. 'It is certain that a significant shift towards cultural and political pluralism will shortly come to Zambia unless a counter Christian culture can pervade.... Light must be a tangible expression of a vibrant faith and in times of difficulty the school must never deviate from the path of trusting Christ and exercising its calling to equip young men and women to serve God well in all aspects of Zambian life.'[2]

The 1995 Report re-emphasised that the Christian foundation of Chengelo is non-denominational and that it recognised that a variety of Christian traditions are represented in the school both at staff and pupil level. For this reason, denominational aspects of the Christian faith are to be approached in a manner so as not to offend or cause disunity. Rather, a balanced approach respectful of the opinions of others is to be encouraged. The Report noted that the school is owned and run by the Mkushi Christian Fellowship Trust Ltd., whose trustees are David Moffat, Russell Wyatt and Barton Young. These three men are also Governors of the school and elders of the MCF.[3] There then follows a classic statement of the middle way pursued by the trustees:

*MCF is an independent non-denominational evangelical conservatively charismatic fellowship and the school could broadly be described as strongly evangelical with an openness to the Spirit of God.*

*As a school we exist to demonstrate unity through diversity.*

The doctrinal position of the school as stated in the 1995 Report is that the Scriptures of the Old and New Testaments are given by inspiration of God and are the final authority and truth and the principal way that God communicates with mankind. The school believes in the Genesis account of creation but accepts that there are various interpretations of this account. The one God is revealed as Father, Son and Holy Spirit. The Lord Jesus Christ is the Saviour of mankind. As a result of the fall man is depraved and is unable to attain to divine righteousness except through Jesus Christ. Jesus Christ is the Head of the Church. The priesthood of all believers is asserted. 'We believe that baptism by immersion is commanded in Scripture so we practise converts/believers' baptism. However we recognise that there are differences of interpretation and practice and respect those beliefs and accept into membership those who hold a different interpretation of baptism. We only baptise minors with parental consent and this is done by the Fellowship.' The Lord's Supper is practised, and the resurrection and the final judgement of all mankind are believed. 'We believe in and allow the operation of the gifts of the Holy Spirit as ordained in Scripture.'[4]

**Charismatic Gifts**
Underlying the 1995 Report was the painful issue of the exercise of charismatic gifts, which interestingly enough did not feature in the MCF Statement of Faith. Chengelo was not unaffected by a deep split in the Brethren movement in Zambia. Gordon Suckling[5] was a leading member of the Brethren who espoused the charismatic

movement and believed in the exercise of the gifts of the Spirit. This was strongly rejected by more traditional members of the Brethren movement, who taught that the gifts of the Spirit had died out with the Apostles and the closing of the canon of Scripture. As Gordon Suckling was the visionary behind Chengelo, the school became suspect in certain quarters, and there was a time when some CMML (Christian Mission in Many Lands) members, and other conservative evangelical missionaries, thought to boycott Chengelo. Gordon Suckling sought a reconciliation with many Brethren from whom he had been separated before he died in 1997. This rapprochement has helped to remove suspicion from Chengelo and made it more widely acceptable within the Christian churches.[6]

Keith and Ida Waddell coming from a reformed Presbyterian background thought at times that there was too much stress upon the charismatic way. 'But ... this was where God had put us and we had to love His Church, His Body at Chengelo, as well as Him. We found our faith grew, was enriched and was strengthened in the fellowship of believers from so many different backgrounds. By the end of our time we felt too that the Church had restored a proper balance between the Gospel and an openness to the Spirit.'[7]

Russell Wyatt affirmed the necessity of maintaining the middle way denominationally. The school has had Pentecostals and a Roman Catholic lady teacher. 'It has been necessary that we should maintain a careful balance. The issue of spiritual gifts has come up. We believe in the manifestation of the Spirit but without undue emphasis on any one specific gift. We have had Fellowship members with completely opposite views about the necessity for tongues.'[8] David Moffat put the matter like this: 'We have had somebody from a pentecostal background, who has pushed very hard to move the MCF in that direction. Then we have had a conservative Evangelical who has gone overboard and tried to get us in the strictly reformed tradition. We have tried very hard to keep the balance that is why we call ourselves Reformed Conservative Charismatics.   There is tension (in this).'[9]

## The Chilongoma Cross
Easter 1991 was a red letter day in the life of Chengelo. On that day the whole school, then numbering 150 pupils, gathered by the wooden cross lying in front of the dining hall. It was the privilege of Form 4 pupils to carry this cross to its special site on top of the Chilongoma Hills. The whole school accompanied the cross on its journey. After three hours scrambling over rocks and around trees, the cross was ready to be erected. That night the pupils sat round a big fire singing for about an hour, before curling up in their sleeping bags in their camp sites on the hills. As Daniela Schempp wrote, 'From school it was exhilarating to see the cross on the hill and to know its significance for Chengelo.'[10]   Seven years later, after the cross had been struck by lightning, the whole school again climbed the hill, and a new cross was erected by David Moffat. As all 300 pupils sat on the summit, the cross was dedicated to the memory of Neil Solomon.

## Compulsory Religion?
Compulsory religion is always an issue in schools. Many feel strongly that Chengelo was set up as a Christian school to shape children into a godly character and to impact the nation for Christ. One parent expressed the need for the children to be equipped spiritually to counteract the effect and influence of Islam. She pointed out that Muslim children are given very specific instruction about their faith. 'If the Muslims are doing that, why should not the Christians.... Children should not be given a choice, I feel, whether or not they go to a discipleship group.... They have to go through a process. If the parents are not willing for their children to undergo this godly training, or the children are not willing, they should be free to leave.'[11]

This attitude is quite common amongst Zambian Christian parents. It contrasts with the voluntarist approach favoured by probably a majority of the expatriate staff, a few of whom may have been put off by the experience of compulsory chapel services in English boarding schools. The current policy is to invite pupils to attend the service run by the Mkushi Christian Community (the new name for the MCF) on a Sunday morning, and to strongly encourage pupils to go to the celebration service, now known as 'Fusion', on a Sunday evening in the school dining hall. A fair number of pupils attend the MCC service, which is held off campus at the thatched open-sided structure opposite the entrance to the school. Many pupils attend 'Fusion', which is an informal prayer and praise worship service, with a substantial student input. Generally a visitor or a staff member is the speaker. Of course there are compulsory elements in the school timetable, such as assemblies and religious studies in the junior forms.

**Discipleship Groups**
In addition, discipleship groups play a large role in Chengelo's life. John Ngulube, who has now been on the staff for fourteen years, has been much involved in discipleship groups and fellowship amongst the young people. He has a background of working with students through Scripture Union, which over the years has been a major Christian influence in the secondary schools of Zambia. John says, 'I see that as my contribution —sharing my faith. I have seen a lot of young people come to faith who are seriously following God since leaving Chengelo.'[12] He explained that discipleship groups are voluntary and that they are largely led by students in Forms 5 and 6. He estimates that 70% of the young people attend discipleship groups.

Very many staff members have greatly contributed to running discipleship groups. Roger Allen said, 'We had many good times. Every Tuesday night we would have the lounge full of maybe forty boys and girls. When we went back in 1997 we had Katie aged three-and-a-half weeks, and she was passed round from pupil to pupil, and straight away for her there was this mix of white and Zambian and Asian.... We would have tremendous weekends away at the Moffat retreat site or Ndubaluba, a tremendous weekend of sharing and praying, teaching and worship. Those were very special times. The Sunday night celebrations were open to any pupils. Two thirds would turn up. And we would all take our turn. I remember one time when John Ngulube had a very sore throat and with literally thirty seconds to go he said, "Roger, I am not going to be able to do it. Would you mind speaking for me." It was the only time that I have stood up to speak without a clue about what I was going to say.' Angie added, 'I just loved the way that they would worship and harmonise.... You worshipped, worked and socialised with the same people. You just had to get on with people from lots of different nations, churches and backgrounds. There were tensions. But somehow God worked it out.'[13]

During their time at Chengelo a good number of staff have been involved in helping out at some of the dozen vernacular churches which come under the umbrella of the Mkushi Christian Community. The Mkushi farming community has grown in recent years largely from an influx of farmers from Zimbabwe. As a result of two Alpha courses run by members of Mkushi Christian Community, a new church was opened known as South Church. Mike Carter, who had taught at Chengelo as Head of Maths and a Deputy-Head, and his wife, Lin, a teacher in the Design and Technology department, were actively involved in the leadership of South Church. After leaving Chengelo, they returned to Mkushi to work exclusively for South Church in a pastoral leadership capacity. A good number of members of the original (North) congregation helped run Alpha groups and home groups. Notable among these are Tony Siddle, one of the two elders, and his wife, Linda, who is Deputy Head of the secondary school. Staff are encouraged to help out in other local churches. Martin Solomon, for example, the Office Manager, and other staff from CMML backgrounds go out and help in some fourteen or so Brethren assemblies in the area.

## Cultural Issues

From time to time issues arose which sometimes generated more heat than light. Alcohol and dress were frequent hot potatoes. Young women teachers could come out from Britain and not realise that their mini-skirts would not be considered appropriate in Zambian eyes, certainly not amongst Christians. Kissing and close physical contact between members of the opposite sex could be misinterpreted in an African context, and Chengelo from its early days laid down clear rules about physical contact between boys and girls. Some Zambian churches, in reaction against the excessive drinking found in the township beerhalls, have a policy of teetotalism.

The matter of the consumption of alcohol by staff came before the Governors in September 1992. The Headmaster stated his intention to refrain from drinking alcohol completely whilst in Zambia. After much discussion, the Governors asked staff to drink alcohol only with the utmost discretion, and to consider a voluntary commitment to abstinence from alcohol whilst at the school. Furthermore, the Board recommended that active instruction be given to the pupils about the dangers of alcohol.

## Pastoral Care

Despite being a Christian school, Chengelo has no chapel and no chaplain. The building of a chapel has been considered from time to time, but it has always been possible to put off a decision on this owing to the shortage of funds. The building of a chapel would raise in quite an acute form the relationship between the school and the Mkushi Christian Community. It would be possible for the school and the Community to diverge and follow different tracks. A chapel would also increase the pressure for a chaplain. In the early days Mike and Beverley Robinson had a significant pastoral role amongst the pupils. In 1995 Roy and Oriel Fellowes, Alison Richardson's parents, came out of retirement to serve at the school. Roy was appointed as a house parent and a religious studies teacher. His pastoral and counselling input to the pupils was very valuable. For many years John Ngulube has been a staff member to whom pupils have turned for counsel and he has been in charge of pastoral affairs for the pupils for some time. John Symons, an experienced Baptist/Brethren pastor, was called to minister to the pastoral needs of members of the MCC North Church, but he has no defined role in the school.

For the main part the pastoral role has been taken up by the Head teachers and houseparents. As the staff are all committed Christians there is a view amongst them that, in addition to their teaching role, they have a pastoral responsibility for the spiritual health of the pupils. This pastoral role is exercised in and out of the classroom and in discipleship groups and other situations. There is a feeling amongst the staff that the appointment of a chaplain would deprive them of their pastoral role, and a fear that such an appointment could take the school down a particular denominational or doctrinal line, which would compromise the middle way so staunchly defended by the founding fathers. The Principal and Head teachers do their best to support the staff pastorally, and the elders of the MCC assist with spiritual matters, but for all these busy people time is limited.

The stress on the staff members is considerable. Neil Solomon is a case in point. Christine Moffat said of Neil: 'He had a very personable style and loved every member of staff and every pupil. But when we got beyond 150 pupils that style could not work and he was getting over-stressed and was having to go off site just to maintain his sanity.'[14] After one year at Ndubaluba, Neil Solomon became ill. His condition steadily deteriorated. He bore his sickness with great fortitude but the cancer finally defeated him.

## Neil Solomon's Memorial Service

A memorial service was held for Neil at Chengelo School on Sunday 19th January 1997. Appreciations were given by Barton Young, Michael Bentley and Ian Richardson. The latter said, 'Because he became a friend to us, a kindred spirit, we feel that we have always known him and we always will. Knowing Neil and being with him has been a blessing, a privilege and an enrichment to our family both spiritually and personally. Amongst other things we all share a love of the hills and mountains.... We climb behind our Guide, who... keeps calling to us to reach "perfection's sacred height". An essential part of any climb is the fellowship on this upward pilgrimage... we were strengthened in our faith and fellowship by being roped with Neil (for this part of the climb).... We could see that Neil was a wee bit higher up the mountain than ourselves and we were blessed by being able to catch a glimpse of Christ from time to time through and yet beyond the man, Neil.'

## Rosemary Mwanakambo and the Chikotis

Neil's departure and later death was undoubtedly a body blow for Chengelo. But the school has had to face a number of very painful bereavements. In June 1999, Rosemary Mwanakombo, the Catering Officer and Kitchen Supervisor, after a short battle with cancer, died. Anne Wyatt paid this tribute: Rosemary 'had a truly serving heart, not only in her work but also in her relationships, and she brought out the best in her kitchen staff and the pupils. Rosemary was the third sister in her close-knit family to die this year, so their loss was even greater than ours, but through it all we saw her shining faith in God.'[15]

The deaths in 2002 of Pastor Joe Chikoti and his wife, Melanie, were a double tragedy for Chengelo. The Chikotis came to Mkushi in 1993, having previously pastored Ndola Christian Fellowship, a large multi-racial church on the Copperbelt. Initially, Joe's involvement was with the church on the Moffats' farm, but his ministry gradually expanded to oversee all the vernacular churches associated with the MCF/MCC. In addition to encouraging the church leaders in prayer and Bible teaching, Joe was also involved in church planting and organising food, clothing, medical supplies and education for the poor. He served as a board member for the Mkushi District Hospital and organised the construction of a school and two health clinics with 'World Servants', a Dutch NGO. Melanie had a significant ministry among the women, conducting conferences for young people, church leaders and married couples. Melanie was killed in a coach crash on her way to Lusaka, and Joe died shortly afterwards following a series of illnesses. The Chikotis left four orphaned children, three of whom, Gloria, Melody and Emmanuel are still at Chengelo. The Governors agreed to guarantee places at the school for the children for a limited time and to review the situation in the light of financial support that might be forthcoming.[16]

**Transformation of Lives**
The greatest reward for the staff and Governors is to see the transformation in the lives of the pupils that can be effected by a living relationship with Jesus Christ. Barton Young said, 'One day David (Moffat) and I were sitting on the grandstand and our first 15 students were being baptised. One of us turned to the other and said, "This is what it is all about." I said that if we can only achieve bringing one or two per cent of our students to the Lord

and we can do this over the years, and those committed students can come into society or the government, then we have arrived at our vision.'[17] Baptism services have been held annually at the school for at least ten years. Candidates have to have the approval of their parents and to complete a course of instruction. Before the baptism they are interviewed about their faith by representatives of the MCC.

David Moffat bears witness to how Chengelo has made a positive impression for good on some of the children. 'There was a girl who was sent to the school, and after two terms a neighbour came along to have a look at Chengelo. This neighbour said he could not believe what a difference the school had had on the relationship between the daughter and her mother. It used to be a very unhappy home situation, and there was much screaming between mother and daughter. But now this has changed completely and the girl has become a really good daughter, and the neighbour wanted to see where this great change had all happened. Then there was another former pupil who seemed to have gone off the rails and disappeared off the horizon. Then suddenly she re-appeared, having gone to study in America. She had done exceptionally well in the United States and had reached a high position in the New York Investment Bank. Now she was also really on fire for the Lord and had given her testimony at the Mkushi Christian Community.'[18]

Russell Wyatt said, 'There have been so many highlights. What the school is all about is young people. To see young people who have come here, some from quite deprived backgrounds, some limited backgrounds, some with no knowledge of God at all, and (to see them) developing in themselves an understanding of themselves and God and his impact on their lives, and the impact that they can have from committing themselves to God. That is the end product.'[19]

## Testimonies

Over the years there have been some wonderful testimonies from the pupils of the work of Christ in their lives:

*Chengelo meant a spiritual awakening that brought about a change in my character. I became more responsible, and began to live the way that a Christian should try to live. My five years at Chengelo led to knowing one vital truth, and that was to serve. To serve in whatever position one holds in life and through serving you learn how to lead people, because you'll know what they want and need.*

*Chengelo meant friendships to me. I made friends — became friends with many people from different races and backgrounds. Whatever our differences, we all learnt how to get on with and accept one another. I made friends who will be friends forever.... They taught me how to laugh and have fun, how to not react to insults whether accidental or intended. I try now to look at incidents from other people's points of views and keep calm. I matured.*

*It was a place where I discovered myself, and I also discovered that I was worth something and I could be a somebody.*

*There is a time for everything; a time to move on, a time when I had to say goodbye to the place where I had experienced secondary school and boarding school; the place where I was saved; the place in which I made real friends; the place where I cried, laughed, grew up —the place that has meant more than I could ever say.*

*Some day I hope I'll come back, to put something back for what I got out of Chengelo. But I don't think I can ever pay it all back. I thank God for blessing me so much in His place —Chengelo. It is a special place.*[20]

The visit in June 1999 of a Navigators team made up jointly of students from the United States and the University of Zambia was a highlight for the many students who made a Christian commitment.

The CET *Newsletter* for December 2000 reported that

15 students had recently been baptised in the school swimming pool. One of the girls who was baptised was Thando Lintini. Here is her testimony: 'I grew up in a Christian home but only gave my life to Jesus in 1995. The past five years have not been easy for me. I lost my mother in 1996 and I really had to struggle because she was the centre of everything that I did. God was with me though and has been very faithful to me, never leaving me or forsaking me. He has been the same God on the mountain that He has been in the valley. Even when I have wandered away and have doubted Him He has still taken care of me and kept me within His reach. Now I want to make a commitment to Him, giving Him everything of the nothing that I am. If anything it was the words of Micah 6:8 that provoked a desire in me to want and get baptised.'[21] In February 2003, 22 young people from Chengelo chose to obey the command of the Lord Jesus Christ and were baptised by Pastor John Symons and Mr John Ngulube.

## Community Service
The practical side of the Christian faith emphasised at Chengelo is community service and the development of a servant heart. This community service takes a variety of forms. Students visit patients in the local hospital, and sometimes buy food for them in the local market. The Anti-Aids Club not only teaches about AIDS but also about love, and the consequences of sex outside marriage. The Club works in the school, the Moffats' workers' compound and in the villages around Nkolonga. Pupils help with the Sunday school in the workers' compound, and organise Christmas parties for the local children. In the compound craft club, Chengelo pupils work together with the local children in painting, making pottery and even producing rugs.

Chengelo pupils also have had opportunities to visit the prison in Mkushi. Ian Richardson reported in the CET *Newsletter* for December 2000: 'A group of students and staff held a service for the prisoners at Mkushi prison. Having developed a good rapport with the prison authorities, they were allowed to meet the prisoners face to face and over 80% responded to the gospel message that was preached.' Charity Namfukwe was a member of the Christian Outreach Team who visited the prison and the hospital: 'There are several memories that I believe I'll remember for a long time: seeing the joy on the faces of the patients who are either temporarily ill or possibly even on their death bed, watching a patient progress from being flat on her back to sitting up and chatting, receiving a warm welcome from prisoners who may never walk the streets as free men again; and reaching out to those less fortunate than ourselves.'[22]

## Mambilima

The development of the link with Mambilima Special School in Luapula Province has been a further opportunity for practical Christianity. Mambilima was an old Brethren mission station in Luapula Province, about nine hours' drive from Chengelo. The special connection between Mambilima and Chengelo began in 1998 when some staff members stumbled across the mission and school while on holiday. At Mambilima, Chengelo students have been involved in painting the hostels, repairing the adventure playground, doing craftwork, physiotherapy, playing sports and evangelistic outreach. The traditional football match between Chengelo and the local team (known affectionately as the Panadolts) is always a big crowd puller. Chengelo students voluntarily raised money for Mambilima and helped to sponsor some Mambilima students to attend an outdoor education programme at Ndubaluba.

Roger Allen remembers with particular poignancy field trips up to Mambilima: 'It was a hospital as well as a school for disabled children. We would go up for five days and live completely hugga-mugga. Some 35 people in a house all hot and sweaty. You would cook over a couple of stoves. Pupils would be doing all sorts of things, building and painting the wards, and taking sport for the kids. After dark we would talk under an African sky, the Mambilima pupils would do a sketch or a song. Then the Chengelo pupils would do something. And you would have all the villagers, perhaps some 600 people, crowding around, and you could see all the faces in the firelight. The fantastic thing was that this was breaking through all sorts of prejudices against disabled people amongst the villagers. I remember the first time the disabled children were laughed at. But each year the respect just grew and grew.'[23] The teachers at Mambilima are remarkable people, sometimes not paid for up to 18 months, and used to having to make their own physiotherapy kits out of their own means and inventiveness. Such visits helped to forge new friendships between Chengelo pupils and highly disadvantaged children.


**Notes**

[1] Chengelo School Audit, Appendix 4, dated October 1995.

[2] The same.

[3] In 1996 MCF became the Mkushi Christian Community.

[4] The same.

[5] The break with the Brethren movement in 1982 led to the founding of the Christian Fellowships (CFZ) of Zambia, which was influenced by the restorationist house church movement of Bryn Jones. The CFZ later split into a number of different groupings.

[6] See *A History of the Christian Brethren in Zambia*, Kovina LK Mutenda, published by Christian Resource Centre, Chingola, Zambia in 2002.

[7] Email to author dated 24.06.05.

[8] Interview with author 17.05.04.

[9] Interview with author 16.05.04.

[10] *Chengelo: The First Three Years*, p. 92.

[11] Mrs Leah Mutala in interview with author 26.05.04.

[12] Interview with author 20.05.04.

[13] Interview with author 19.03.04.

[14] Interview with author 16.05.04.

[15] *Chengelo Educational Trust Newsletter*, December 1999.

[16] *Chengelo Educational Trust Newsletter*, July 2002.

[17] Interview with author 19.05.04.

[18] Interview with author 16.05.04.

[19] Interview with the author May 2004.

[20] *Chengelo Educational Trust Newsletter*, July 1995.

[21] *Chengelo Educational Trust Newsletter*, No 13, December 2000.

[22] *Chengelo Educational Trust Newsletter*, No 15, February 2002.

[23] Interview with author 19.03.04.

# Chapter Twelve

# The Future

## A New Team Takes Over

This book is being written at a critical time in the history of Chengelo School. The school is moving from a period of birth and childhood to adulthood and maturity. Putting it another way, Chengelo is developing from the creative building phase to the period of consolidation and maintenance. In the life of any institution this transition is a difficult one.

At the same time Chengelo is about to make that transition with an entirely new leadership team. Alison Richardson has stood down as Headteacher of the primary school and Keith Waddell her deputy is also leaving to move to a post elsewhere in Zambia. Alison's place is being taken by Steve Jordan, who comes with 23 years' experience as a primary teacher, including five years as a deputy head, in the UK. Tim Sims, the Head of the secondary school, is leaving Chengelo after a distinguished and dynamic career in which he has implanted his strong academic and spiritual values to the school. He is to be replaced by Andrew Cowling, who has been Deputy Head at Chengelo for the past two years, having taught earlier in a large comprehensive in England.

Most significantly of all, Ian and Alison Richardson are saying farewell to Chengelo after fourteen and a half years. The school has changed out of all recognition over these years. When the Richardsons arrived there were 100 pupils and 12 staff. Today there are nearly 400 pupils and 80 staff. Ian remembers Neil Solomon telling him in those early days that the school could not offer English literature because it could not afford the textbooks, which needed to be changed every three years. Over the past nine years Ian has presided over the school at a time of unprecedented building and growth. During the Richardson incumbency, Chengelo has reached great heights of academic achievement and sporting success. Ian and Alison are moving to a new Christian Academy at Doncaster in the North of England, where Ian will be deputy head of a school of 1450 pupils. In their final letter to school parents Ian and Alison profess their confidence in the future. 'We know that we leave Chengelo in safe hands; not just of the new leadership team, but in God's own hands. In the words of the apostle Paul we are, "confident of this, that he who began a good work in you will carry it on to completion until the day of Christ Jesus."'[1] They will be sorely missed.

Ian Richardson's departure as Principal at the end of 2004 has opened the way to a new appointment, that of Head of Staff Development. The post is going to Jani Zabangwa. Jani's previous experience includes being Principal of Mukinge Girls' High School in Kasempa and teaching at Mpelembe School, where he was also responsible for counselling and guidance in all the ZCCM schools. More recently he has worked as the Training Manager and HIV/AIDS and Transformation Officer at the Christian Enterprise Trust of Zambia in Kitwe. Jani Zabangwa is a committed Christian and an elder at Nkana East Brethren Assembly. Jani will take responsibility for staff development and external relations at Chengelo. In making the appointment the Governors expressed their confidence that the triumvirate of Jani Zabangwa, Andrew Cowling and Steve Jordan could take Chengelo forward in the new phase of its existence. In January 2005 it was decided to make Martin Solomon Head of Business Administration and Financial Control, of equal standing with the other three heads. There will certainly be great challenges for this new team to work harmoniously together and not to lose sight of the original vision.

## How Far Has Chengelo Achieved Its Vision?

At this juncture in the life of Chengelo it is pertinent to ask how far the school has achieved and lived up to that vision on which it is founded. The first aim of that vision was to establish a high quality secondary school on a Christian basis to meet an urgent need in Zambia. There can be little doubt that Chengelo is recognised today throughout Zambia as an excellent school. Its first-class academic results in the IGSCE examinations speak for themselves. The school has not only unrivalled sporting facilities in Zambia but its repeated success in the ISAZ trophy shows that it has put those facilities to good use. Its outdoor education at Ndubaluba is unique in Zambia.

But has the school fulfilled its purpose to cater for the children of key Christian workers? One of the criticisms, which can be made of a school like Chengelo, is that it is an elitist school catering for the children of wealthy parents. In response it can be said that the consistent aim of the Board is that 10% of the children at Chengelo should be on assisted places. In 1997 some 32 children were receiving assistance from bursaries without which they would not have been able to attend Chengelo. In 2001 25% of children were on asssisted places, 10.7% of pupils were the children of missionaries, and 12.6% of pupils were the children of Zambian full-time Christian workers. In addition a need for financial assistance can arise suddenly when a parent of a pupil dies. Death is no stranger to Zambia because the AIDS pandemic has cut lethal swathes through all classes of society. In such an event the school tries to ensure that the child can complete his or her education at Chengelo.

Chengelo has endeavoured to keep its fees as low as possible. The Principal claims that compared with other private schools which offer an international curriculum, only Banani School, a girls-only school, run by the Bahai faith, is cheaper by a few hundred dollars.

*Our boarding fees are the same or cheaper than the day fees at other international schools.... The main reason that we can subsidise the fees is that our teaching staff take a reduced salary by international standards. We are expensive because the whole boarding side costs a lot of money and we are remote and spend a lot of money on transport and food, etc.*

*Other schools will be offering staff salaries which are three times what ours are.... We do have problems with appointing some local staff because our salaries are lower. This is particularly so with Zambian staff who have been working elsewhere, such as in Botswana. For example, Martin Solomon was employed in Botswana on expatriate terms, but he and his wife, Kukeña, were prepared to take a big cut in conditions and move back because they felt that God was calling them here.*[2]

The second aim of the Governors in setting up the school was that it should be a means of outreach for Christ into the community at large. The Governors and staff have not backed away from their determination to make Chengelo a Christian school in its ethos and its teaching. When assessing the vision in 1997, Ian Richardson wrote that one of the distinguishing features of Chengelo is that Christian activities are integrated into the main school programme. In that year the school followed the Alpha course, with 200 pupils voluntarily attending the Sunday evening celebrations, which were followed up in the weekly discipleship courses. In writing testimonials for Form 5 pupils, he was encouraged to note that at least 12 had become Christians whilst at Chengelo, and that two-thirds of the year group were able to testify to a growth in their faith during their time at Chengelo. Pupils had acted as counsellors at a local youth conference. During a sports fixture one pupil was able to share the gospel with a teacher from the visiting side. In previous years he has known whole families coming to know the Lord: first the children at the school and then the parents through the children.[3] The video of Chengelo shown on national television, the examination successes of the school, its sporting prowess, and its touring productions in Lusaka and the Copperbelt have all put Chengelo on the map in Zambia, and enabled its light for Christ to shine out in the nation.

## How Can Old Chengelians Impact the Nation?

The third aim of Chengelo was that the school would be a landmark for Christ and Christian principles. It was hoped that the school would produce future leaders in all sections of Zambian society, in business, government and the church. In 1997 Ian Richardson acknowledged that it was too early to see the fulfilment of this objective. He did, however, point to the example of Chris Mutale in leading Christian students at the Copperbelt University and in taking ministry teams into local churches, and of Tanzya Chisambo who had joined the staff of the primary school as an assistant houseparent. There are a number of other Chengelians making their mark in Zambia. But the hard truth of the matter is that a large number of former pupils are now studying abroad or working outside Zambia. How many are going to return to Zambia and contribute to its development? When the Chengelo Educational Trust met at the Zambian High Commission in London in October 2002, the High Commissioner, Mr SK Mubukwana, posed the question: How successful was Chengelo in keeping its graduates in Zambia?[4]

217

When John Ngulube, who has now taught for fourteen years at Chengelo and has resisted offers to go elsewhere, was asked how Zambian graduates can be encouraged to stay in Zambia, he answered: 'I think as Zambian staff we should be talking to students to stay in the country to build the nation. This cannot be done by expatriates. We should be giving pupils pride in their country and see if they can invest in the country once they start working. It is very difficult. Maybe the message should be, if need be, go and make money elsewhere, but then invest that money in Zambia and come back and try to make a difference. Christians do have a responsibility to nation building.... We are fulfilling the vision in regard to providing education but there is still a lot of room in improving the whole area of leadership training and in persuading people to be patriotic enough to come back and help this nation. Maybe we need people from the political sphere and the churches coming to address the students.'[5]

On the issue of students going overseas, Russell Wyatt commented: 'Chengelo is well-known across the country and what it stands for. What its impact is only time will tell. It is a disappointment that so many former students go overseas and find employment there. It was not the intention of Chengelo that it should be a gateway out of the country. But it is very difficult to achieve that because the aspirations set here are very high and it is not always possible to achieve those within Zambia. The hope is that some of these youngsters will come back, especially since the family ties are very strong in the African community.'[6] Christine Moffat also expressed the view that it would take another ten to fifteen years before Old Chengelians would emerge to take national leadership roles in Zambia, but already she noted that some were returning to Zambia after ten or more years abroad.[7]

Another governor, Mpundu Mutala, the General Secretary of the Zambian Bible Society, had this point of view: 'How do you judge students who have gone overseas? You cannot blame them.... You cannot judge or measure everything over such a short time.... I think that it is emerging in a small way. Many of them are still in their mid- twenties. But they may think differently when they are in their thirties....' So far as recruiting Zambians to teach at Chengelo, Mpundu suggested: 'Specifically we would need to revisit the salary structure and conditions of service. But they must also feel the sense of the call of God. Many are [at Chengelo] because they responded to a challenge to teach in a Christian school.... We should emphasise more the discipleship basis of service. Some may feel called to go to Chengelo.'[8]

When the author dined with a group of fifth and sixth form girls in May 2004, he was impressed by their maturity and their respect for the school and its Christian ethos. One of the girls had an ambition to be President of Zambia. She had a clear idea of what her manifesto platform would contain. She would aim to get rid of poverty and corruption, to introduce free education, to reduce the number of government ministers, to remove children from the streets and to establish a truly Christian government.[9] Who knows whether Chengelo will produce Zambia's first woman President? During this visit, when members of the Chengelo Educational Trust held career talks for pupils, another striking feature was how many of the girls seemed to want a business career. If girls generally are less venal than men, this might augur well for business ethics and morality in the world of commerce.

That part of the vision which focuses on the impact of Chengelo students on the nation of Zambia will take time for its fulfilment. It may be necessary at the present time for many Chengelians to pursue education and employment overseas, but the hope is that they will return to repay something of what they owe to Chengelo and to Zambia. Clearly it is important that Chengelo students are given good career advice and informed of the opportunities that there are within Zambia. It must also be the hope that economic conditions will allow companies and organisations within Zambia to offer improved salaries and conditions. But the ultimate issue for Zambian Christians is to develop that servant heart which calls them to serve God and their neighbour within their native land.

## Some Current Issues

There are a number of other issues, which confront the school Governors at this time. They are the recruitment of local staff, a teacher training college and the membership of the Board of Governors. During Ian Richardson's tenure as Headmaster/Principal, Chengelo has moved from a situation where a minority of the teaching staff were Zambian to one where over 50% of the teaching staff is now Zambian. The administrative staff is all Zambian. In the past senior management was largely expatriate, but now the four joint heads are balanced between two expatriates, Andrew Cowling and Steve Jordan, and two Zambians, Jani Zabangwa and Martin Solomon.

In the matter of teacher recruitment, is it better for Chengelo to keep a mixture of Zambian and expatriate staff? The Governors tend to believe that having teachers from other countries enriches the school. They cite the desire of various Zambian parents for a substantial expatriate teaching input at Chengelo. They also point to the experience of schools in other countries who have found a 40/60 % expats/nationals ratio of staff ensures the advantage of both worlds. The policy on staff recruitment has been to source the expertise which will ensure that the highest academic standards are maintained and to select the best person for the job. If there are two candidates equally qualified, then the preference is to appoint the Zambian. This policy allows the make-up of the teaching staff to evolve over time.

One of the ways used to help promote Zambian staff has been the encouragement for them to do master's courses.

The school is promoting the MBA course in educational management run by Leicester University. Currently five Zambians are doing this course. Attracting high quality staff, both local and expatriate, at all levels in the school is a constant challenge for Chengelo. As Bob Baker put it, 'The strength of the first fifteen is frequently to be found in a strong well-motivated second fifteen.'[10]

## Should Chengelo Go Into Tertiary Education?

Another way favoured by those who want to see committed Christians teaching at Chengelo and other schools in Zambia is to advocate the establishment of a teacher training college attached to the school. Others are fearful that to go into tertiary education would be a bridge too far for Chengelo, and that it would overstretch the resources and the goodwill that attach to the school. But Mpundu Mutala is one governor who favours such a move. He puts the case like this: 'Now we are faced with the challenge of post-secondary education, my own children are struggling with this. If Chengelo is facing the issue of recruiting staff, we see the students who have gone through Chengelo as forming a backbone for the future teaching staff in Chengelo. But we cannot do that if Chengelo does not look into the options. We have set up the sixth form. We have looked into providing some training programme for teachers to upgrade their level of teaching... so that they can be fitted into teaching at Chengelo. There is also the possibility of setting up an actual teacher training college... in collaboration with other institutions. This would be too large for Chengelo to go it alone. We would need to network. There are already talks with other groups, other churches, who want to set up a university. Chengelo could buy into it or spearhead it. In that way we would be dealing with the problem of losing students who have gone through Chengelo. Because once they go overseas it is difficult to bring them back.... We want to excite children about what they can do for their own country. But it is hard to do this outside the country. If they have a negative picture ... then it will be difficult to bring them back.'[11]

## The Board of Governors

Before considering the composition of the Board of Governors, proper tribute needs to be paid to the vision, faith, commitment, industry and resilience of the founding fathers and their wives. Some years ago affectionate pen portraits of the three couples appeared in the CET *Newsletter*. David Moffat is highly regarded for his deep commitment to the nation and people of Zambia, which was acknowledged by the local MP when he referred to him as Mr Mkushi. How would you recognise Mr Mkushi Moffat? 'The answer is to look out for an extremely old Range Rover with its back cut off. Inside the cab the bearded and bespectacled farmer sporting one of those shirts that Christine has failed to get him to part with, or the bright green pullover (essential part of this winter's fashion collection). Slobbering behind comes his constant companion – Shaka the Rottweiler – he's a big softie really.'[12]

If David Moffat is the shaker, Christine is the perfect team player and completer-finisher. Christine is the one who keeps the notes and ensures that the 'i's are dotted and the 't's crossed. 'She shares with David an earnestness about seeking God through prayer and a desire to let Him have his way.'[13] In addition to her work as Secretary to the Board of Governors, Christine is much involved in the two health clinics, which look after the workers at Chengelo School and at the Moffat farm. She buys the medicines and keeps a sharp eye on the stores. As the nearest government school is six miles away, the Moffats, together with the Wyatts and Chengelo School, have also set up a school (Kapanda School) for farm workers, to which they and others put in money for each child entered by them. Christine does the wages, the National Pension

Scheme contributions and the PAYE. When it is put to her that life would have been much easier if the Moffats had just stuck to farming, she says, 'It would have been less hard work but very boring. It has been hard work but very enjoyable.'[14]

Russell Wyatt, who has been Chairman of Governors since the beginning, is the doyen of the Board, a steady hand at the tiller, whose wisdom and experience is much valued. He bears testimony to, '...seeing the hand of God at work in bringing the right staff to the school at just the right time, and providing the resources required just when they were needed. It is the Lord's doing and it is marvellous in our eyes!'[15] 'Auntie Anne', as Russell's wife is almost universally called, is his stalwart better half. She has often shouldered the responsibility of overseeing the catering between catering officers. 'Anne recalls the many tins of vegetables sent by Norman Lane (of Medical Missionary News) – the ravioli seemed to go on for ever! A large responsibility Anne has taken on is the recruiting and training of domestic workers who work in the houses and the laundries (sixty at present). This provides much needed work for local families. Added to this is the furnishing and preparation of houses for staff and the distribution of clothing to needy families in local villages. As somebody has said, "Anne is everybody's mother and many staff and pupils would verify this."'

The third of the founding families are Barton and Yvonne Young. 'Barton is every inch the Zambian farmer, with his open, tanned and weather-beaten face with iron handshake to match. Here is a face that has gazed on many seasons, endured many days of baking heat and watched many skies for signs of the weather. He clearly loves farming and outdoor life in general. Zambia's answer to John Wayne, he quickly warms to people, as they do to him, his craggy features fast melting into warm, kind smiles.'[16] Yvonne is the perfect hostess who loves hospitality and making people feel at home. She shares in many of the school's activities. 'Her passionate love of children is seen in her keen participation in the primary school's Sunday worship (known as King's Kids) and in her devotion to her grandchildren who relish her visits.'

All the founding governors would be the first to admit that they are now rather long in the tooth. Bringing new and younger blood into the membership of the Board is an issue that greatly concerns the Governors.[17] It is, however, very hard to find committed Christians with the maturity, the time and the energy to sit on the Board. David Moffat says tongue in cheek, 'Senile decay is rapidly catching up with us.' But he continues in characteristically blunt terms. 'We would be happy to hand over to others, especially local people, who would be prepared to be committed to the vision.[18] And the people that we would like to take over, and there are plenty of them, are so overwhelmed with other responsibilities that they are reluctant to get involved.... Amongst the Mkushi farmers there are some fine farmers from Zimbabwe who would be ideal but they are just starting their farms and there is no way that they could do it yet.... I have no desire to hang on to the baby. I would have thrown out the baby with the bath-water long ago.'[19]

## Where Does Chengelo Go From Here?

So where does Chengelo go from here? The School Development Plan: 2003-2007 has plenty of initiatives in mind, including priorities for 2003, and medium-term objectives for 2004-07. These latter include for the primary school the introduction of gymnastics, the development of special needs resources, and the holding of a Bible week with a full-time children's worker. For the secondary school, it is envisaged implementing a reviewed curriculum for Forms 1-5; considering a vocational course and alternatives to A-levels in the sixth form; developing annual exchanges with French-speaking students; introducing the equipment for pottery making in the DT

Centre; establishing four tennis courts and three netball courts; developing the music with better equipment and new instruments; building closer links with local churches; taking pupils on evangelistic and outreach teams; having an environmental education centre at Ndubaluba; phasing out wood-fired boilers and replacing them with electric geysers. There is also a need for another science laboratory. The single biggest project would be the construction of a main school hall. This could be used for assemblies, as well as badminton, basketball and five-a-side football. It might also incorporate a music studio. Alternatively a Creative Arts Centre might be built including a music studio. Clearly Chengelo does not intend to rest on its laurels.

The potential impact of Chengelo on Zambia and indeed upon Africa is enormous. The future of Chengelo lies in the hands of Almighty God and in those of his servants who are ready to run with the original vision for the school. Let a parent have the last word:

*All five of my children have been through Chengelo. We have followed all the developments at Chengelo from its inception and we are very thrilled at the development of a Christian school with the emphasis on shaping future leaders of our country, shaping them into godly character and the fear of God, which our nation desperately needs.... As a parent, who is a Christian, I would love the school to continue to get many children from Christian parents. I know that there is a challenge as to who goes to Chengelo, maybe the one who has the ability to pay. The vision of Chengelo was to raise godly pupils who would impact our nation.... Why start a Christian school? It was a burden that Christian parents had for their children not to be influenced by the world. Yes, they are in the world but they are going to school to learn godly values. Be equipped academically, but at the same time keep that spiritual focus and let it be engraved in them and be a part of them....*

*Chengelo is a tremendous school. From the first time*

*when the trustees met until now, it is incredible what God
has done and we want to thank the Lord for that.*

*I personally feel very passionate and jealous about
Chengelo and its vision. I want it to be maintained from
the beginning what it was. And as a Zambian I want the
children from Chengelo to impact this nation....*

*Final thoughts. I think that we want to encourage the
teachers and the Board of Governors.... A number of them
have sacrificed greatly and have poured their lives into the
life of the school. We just want to pray that God will bless
them and will continually remind them of the original vision;
that this will not depart from their eyes.*[20]

Unless the LORD builds the house,
its builders labour in vain.

*Psalm 127:1*

**Notes**

[1] Letter to parents dated 1 December 2004.

[2] Interview with author 18.05.04.

[3] *Chengelo Educational Trust Newsletter*, No 7, 1997.

[4] A new initiative by CET has just been announced as
this book goes to press. It is to establish Post-Chengelo
Scholarships. 'This new enterprise aims to provide an
incentive for recent former Chengelo pupils to engage in a
project of their own design that will assist them to use their
learning within the working environment of Zambia where
they would have to commit themselves for two years.' Dr
Peter Green in *Imbila*, No. 23, December, 2005.

[5] Interview with author 20.05.04.

[6] Interview with author 19.05.04.

[7] Interview with author 16.05.04.

[8] Interview with author 26.05.04.

[9] Natashya Ngona at school dinner on 14.15.04.

[10] Note to author attached to email dated 07.02.05.

[11] Interview with author 26.05.04.

[12] *Chengelo Educational Trust Newsletter*, No 8, 1998. Shaka

died two years ago and has been replaced by Toby, half Rottweiler, half Alsatian.

[13] Ibid.

[14] Interview with author 16.05.04.

[15] *Chengelo Educational Trust Newsletter*, No 11, 1999.

[16] *Chengelo Educational Trust Newsletter*, No 9, 1999.

[17] The current Board of Governors consists of Russell Wyatt (Farmer), Harold Rea (Consultant Metallurgist, Mopani Copper Mine), David Moffat (Farmer), Barton Young (Farmer), Traugott Hartmann (Missionary), Felix Muchimba (Principal GLO Discipleship Training Centre, Ndola), Mpundu Mutala (General Secretary, Bible Society of Zambia), Gladys Mutungu (Office Manager, Professional Insurance, Lusaka), Paddy Mutwale (Organising Secretary Family Life Ministries, Lusaka), Andy Patching (Missionary, Director ISUBILO Care Ministry), Peter Pedersen (Senior Missionary, Apostolic Church in Zambia).

[18] The established criteria for a Chengelo Governor are: '(1) A committed believer in, and visible follower of, Jesus Christ the Divine Son of God. (2) One who accepts and fully believes in the ethos of the school. (3) One who understands the Bye-Laws and Aims, Standards and Guidelines of the Board of Governors. (4) One who is prepared to commit themselves long-term to the interests and needs of the school, to such an extent that they may be called at times to give priority and loyalty to the school over and above their other interests and responsibilities. The preferences are for a person who (a) has leadership and management experience; (b) has a personal interest in the school; (c) has experience in the educational field; (d) is in good standing in the Christian community of Zambia and in either the professional or business community.'

[19] Interview with author 16.05.04.

[20] Mrs Leah Mutala in interview with author 26.05.04.

# Postscript

**Chengelo in 2005 and Beyond...**

When Jesus said, "I am the vine; you are the branches" (John 15:5a), he described a living and breathing organism that would represent the people of God. Chengelo School aims to be this living breathing organism, for whom the process of change is and will be ongoing. God was not just the creator of the vision all those years ago. God is the creative vision and the internal dynamic of an organism that has become an institution, but is far more than just this.

Ask the staff who serve here and they will tell you their testimony of how God led them to Chengelo. So many testimonies all showing one central truth. It is God's hand upon Chengelo that has created it all the way along its journey. If Chengelo was the work of man alone it would have failed long ago. Leading an organism of this nature requires continual reflection —seeing the people God draws to His purposes and discerning their gifts and seeing how God can use them for His glory. Like all institutions we talk of development plans, staff training, vision statements, appraisals targets and objectives. All these must be viewed through the dynamic of God's hand upon Chengelo and His guidance. In practice this creates an organism that is wanting to push doors and try new things. It creates an organism that has a fluid structure to it and is not tied down in its organisational approach. It is no coincidence that this approach has built one of the most successful schools in Zambia, if not the most successful.

This book is a testimony to many of those who gave of themselves to help fulfil part of this vision. In January 2005 four new Heads took on the joint leadership of Chengelo School. Martin Solomon had been with Chengelo as the Office Manager but has now stepped up to Head of Business and Finance, Andrew Cowling had been with the school as the Deputy Headteacher of Secondary and now has stepped up to Headteacher of Secondary, Jani Zabangwa was new to Chengelo and took up the role of Head of Staff Development and External Relations and Steve Jordan, who arrived in August 2004, has taken up his role as Headteacher of Primary. There was a real sense in which a new era was beginning in the life of Chengelo.

As we draw to the end of 2005 we give thanks to God for all that He has made possible. The school continues to mature as a physical site with modernisation programmes in almost every area of the school from electrification to plumbing, from the hostels to the classrooms. We see the vision of future leaders being further developed through the beginnings of a new prefect structure and with the introduction of a Head Boy and Head Girl to Chengelo. We see the first class standards being raised in the school performances, music concerts, sports competitions, public speaking events, horse riding shows. We see the development of Christian commitment from Chengelo's own CIA (Christians in Action) which has enabled students to mature in their faith through leadership in discipleship groups, leadership in worship, and a brave few are even leading in preaching. 2005 saw the first meeting of the Chengelo Association developing links with former students, helping us to follow up on the impact of the vision. We hope and pray that the Association continues to grow in strength.

The original vision that was given to the Founders of Chengelo, and that has inspired teachers, administrators, parents, workers of all sorts, from all over the world to come and serve God's purposes here at Chengelo, lives on. It lives on through the lives of those who now call Chengelo their school and even their home. It lives on through the lives, through the commitment, but most of all through the love of God that pours out through each of us as we worship Him in our actions. This history is a testimony of some of those lives. It reflects some of the problems faced, some of the challenges that had to be confronted. There will always be challenges. When we get things right we can give glory to God. When we get things wrong we must accept, humbly, the responsibility ourselves. As we look forward, which we do with eagerness, we will 'fear God' but also 'trust Him'. Above all else we must do as we are commanded to do in Matthew 22:34–40. We must love God with all our heart and soul and mind, and we must love our neighbour as our self. For if we can do this we will obey all that our Lord commands and we may truly be a 'witness to the light'.

Andrew Cowling

*Chengelo School*
*October 2005*

# Appendix 1
## Staff List
### *in date order of appointment*

| | From | To | Subjects/posts |
|---|---|---|---|
| Mrs Barbara Rushby | 03/1988 | 02/2001 | Book-keeper |
| Mr Keith Rushby | 03/1988 | 02/2001 | Buyer, administrative assistant |
| Mrs Ruby Braumann | 05/1988 | 07/1994 | Biology, Geography |
| Mr Neil Solomon | 05/1988 | 12/1993 | Headmaster |
| Mr David Rust | 07/1988 | 08/1992 | History, Art, Deputy Head |
| Mrs Rachel Rust | 07/1988 | 08/1992 | Mathematics |
| Mrs Michelle Cantlay | 09/1988 | | Food science, I.T. |
| Mrs Gita George | 09/1988 | 12/1989 | Nurse |
| Mr Keith George | 09/1988 | 12/1989 | Geography |
| Mrs Floridah Mutambo | 09/1988 | | English, Book-keeper |
| Mrs Anne Wyatt | 09/1988 | | Domestic supervisor |
| Mrs Diana Parker-Dennison | 01/1989 | | Stables, Librarian |
| Miss Doreen Brown | 06/1989 | 06/1990 | catering |
| Miss Norma Grenzenburg | 09/1989 | 08/1990 | Primary |
| Mr Neville Pietersen | 09/1989 | 06/1990 | Builder, hostel parent |
| Mrs Robi Pietersen | 09/1989 | 06/1990 | Admin assistant, librarian |
| Mr Mike Robinson | 09/1989 | 08/1992 | Hostel parent, P.E. |
| Mrs Anne Godfrey | 01/1990 | 12/1992 | English, Music, Hostel parent |
| Mr John Ngulube | 01/1990 | | Maths |
| Mr Mike Mahaffey | 09/1990 | 12/1992 | Builder |
| Mrs Robyn Mahaffey | 09/1990 | 12/1992 | Nurse |
| Mr Evans Mbozi | 09/1990 | 08/1992 | French |
| Mrs Kabaenda Mbozi | 09/1990 | 08/1992 | |
| Mrs Alison Richardson | 09/1990 | 12/2004 | Primary Teacher, Religious Studies, Primary Head |
| Mr Ian Richardson | 09/1990 | 12/2004 | Chemistry, Head Secondary, Principal |
| Miss Anne Carrington | 02/1991 | 12/1995 | H.M.'s secretary, hostel parent |
| Mrs Anne Bentley | 01/1992 | 12/1998 | Domestic supervisor |
| Mr Brian Bentley | 01/1992 | 12/1998 | Office Manager |
| Mrs Bronwyn Mutton | 01/1992 | 12/1994 | I.T. |
| Mr Les Mutton | 01/1992 | 12/1994 | Science |
| Mr Mark Newhouse | 01/1992 | 12/1994 | Maths |
| Mrs Mwaka Ngulube | 01/1992 | | volunteer, KPS teacher, accounts assistant |
| Mr John Smiles | 02/1992 | 12/1993 | Builder |
| Mrs Marise Smiles | 02/1992 | 12/1993 | French |
| Ms Mildred Mayaba | 07/1992 | 06/1995 | caterer |

| | | | |
|---|---|---|---|
| Mrs Angie Allen | 09/1992 | 07/1994 | Primary houseparent |
| Mr Roger Allen | 09/1992 | 07/1994 | History, Development Studies |
| Mr Keesjan Van der Maas | 09/1992 | 04/1997 | Agriculture |
| Mrs Reinette Van der Maas | 09/1992 | 04/1997 | Hostel parent |
| Mrs Jane Guest | 01/1993 | 12/1994 | Religious Studies |
| Mr Peter Guest | 01/1993 | 12/1994 | Hostel parent, Religious Studies |
| Mr David Hill | 01/1993 | | Maths, Hostel parent |
| Mr Rob Prentice | 01/1993 | 04/1997 | Art teacher |
| Mrs Denise Sims | 02/1993 | 12/2004 | Biology, Geography |
| Mr Tim Sims | 02/1993 | 12/2004 | Geography, Head 6th Form, Head Secondary |
| Mr Celestine Chitalu | 05/1993 | 01/1997 | Builder |
| Mr Andrew Thomas | 05/1993 | 07/1995 | History |
| Mrs Louise Thomas | 05/1993 | 12/1996 | English |
| Ms Evelyn Howes | 08/1993 | 07/1998 | Receptionist |
| Mrs Linda Siddle | 11/1993 | | French, Pastoral, Deputy Head |
| Mr Tony Siddle | 11/1993 | 08/2004 | Training Farm Manager |
| Mrs Inonge Chifuka | 01/1994 | 10/2003 | Geography |
| Mr Nelson Chifuka | 01/1994 | 10/2003 | Mathematics |
| Mr Mike Hackston | 01/1994 | 12/1998 | Biology |
| Mrs Val Hackston | 01/1994 | 12/1998 | HM's P.A. |
| Mr Timothy Cripps | 09/1994 | 12/1996 | Workshop supervisor |
| Miss Kathy Haigh | 09/1994 | 07/1998 | I.Y.A co-ordinator, History, houseparent |
| Mr Richard Thompson | 09/1994 | | Geography, Outdoor Education, I..Y.A. |
| Mrs Ida Waddell | 09/1994 | 07/2004 | nurse |
| Mr Keith Waddell | 09/1994 | 07/2004 | Primary teacher, Deputy Head |
| Mr Timothy Foster | 01/1995 | 12/1996 | Sports |
| Mr Abraham Mazyopa | 01/1995 | 01/2001 | Lab. Technician & Reprographics |
| Mr John Mellen | 01/1995 | 12/1999 | Maths, Zongwe hostel parent, Tech. D., engineer |
| Mrs Ruth Mellen | 01/1995 | 12/1999 | Zongwe hostel parent |
| Mrs Barbara Thomson | 01/1995 | 09/2002 | Primary teacher |
| Mr Chris Meyer | 02/1995 | 12/1996 | Hostel Parent |
| Mrs JenniMeyer | 02/1995 | 12/1996 | |
| Mrs Rachel Bentley | 09/1995 | 12/1998 | Primary teacher |
| Mrs Lin Carter | 09/1995 | 08/2002 | Hostel parent, textiles, special needs |
| Mr Michael Carter | 09/1995 | 08/2002 | Mathematics, Deputy Head |
| Mrs Rosemary Mwanakombo | 09/1995 | 04/1999 | Caterer |
| Mr Eddie Smith | 09/1995 | 12/1998 | Science |
| Mrs Mary Smith | 09/1995 | 12/1998 | Primary Teacher |

| | | | |
|---|---|---|---|
| Mrs Julia Nolan | 11/1995 | 03/2002 | Primary Teacher |
| Mr Melvyn Nolan | 11/1995 | 03/2002 | Primary Head |
| Mr Nicholas Holt | 01/1996 | 04/1998 | English |
| Mr John Thornberry | 01/1996 | 04/1997 | architect |
| Mrs Rachel Thornberry | 01/1996 | 04/1997 | Primary teacher |
| Mrs Caroline Snook | 04/1996 | 04/1997 | Hostel parent |
| Mr Don Snook | 04/1996 | 04/1997 | Hostel parent |
| Mr Ng'ambilani Lungu | 09/1996 | 12/2003 | Careers, Bemba, Exam Officer |
| Mrs Laurinda Miles Rudge | 09/1996 | 08/2002 | French, English, hostel parent, deputy head |
| Mr Joe Musonda | 12/1996 | 03/2002 | Workshop supervisor |
| Mrs Niya Musonda | 12/1996 | 12/2002 | Accounts Assistant |
| Mrs Jean Lungu | 01/1997 | 12/2003 | Accounts Assistant |
| Miss Megan Richardson | 01/1997 | 05/2001 | P.E. |
| Mrs Hilda Tembo | 01/1997 | | Nurse |
| Mr Saul Tembo | 01/1997 | | Art teacher |
| Mr Edward Chitembo | 02/1997 | 12/2003 | Agricultural Science |
| Mrs Elaine Richardson | 05/1997 | 12/2001 | Primary teacher |
| Mr Laurence Richardson | 05/1997 | 12/2001 | English |
| Mr James Brookman | 09/1997 | 07/1999 | Physics |
| Mrs Anne Elledge | 09/1997 | | Primary hostel parent, teacher |
| Mr Philip Elledge | 09/1997 | | Geography, English |
| Mr Jon Stamford | 09/1997 | 12/1999 | P.E., History |
| Mrs Sarah Stamford | 09/1997 | 12/1999 | Science |
| Miss Becky Thorman | 09/1997 | 12/2001 | stables, hostel parent |
| Mrs Maureen Mazyopa | 01/1998 | 12/2001 | Accounts Assistant |
| Mrs Angela Pizey | 01/1998 | 12/1998 | primary |
| Mr Mark Pizey | 01/1998 | 12/1998 | hostel parent |
| Mr Chriss Banda | 03/1998 | | Librarian, Hostel Parent |
| Mrs Martha Banda | 03/1998 | | Secretary to Primary Head |
| Miss Mirriam Nakufa | 09/1998 | 10/2003 | Nurse |
| Miss Prisca Nakufa | 09/1998 | | Pre-school teacher |
| Miss Angela Nyambe | 09/1998 | | Receptionist |
| Mr Martin Solomon | 09/1998 | | Business Manager |
| Mr Andrew Astington | 01/1999 | 07/2000 | History |
| Mrs Chris Astington | 01/1999 | 07/2000 | Primary Teacher |
| Mr Philip Pike | 01/1999 | 07/2001 | Site Manager |
| Mrs Liz Polley | 01/1999 | 12/2001 | Assistant, Pre-school teacher |
| Mrs Kukenga Solomon | 01/1999 | | Geography, Head of Humanities |
| Mr Chabi Chondoka | 05/1999 | 07/2001 | Sports trainee/teacher, house parent |
| Miss Hannah Flanders | 09/1999 | 05/08 | Biology teacher, hostel parent |
| Mrs Mulambwa Gondwe | 09/1999 | 08/2004 | Primary teacher |
| Mr Martin Loy | 09/1999 | 03/2000 | |

| | | | |
|---|---|---|---|
| Mrs Wendy Loy | 09/1999 | 03/2000 | Hostel parent |
| Miss Claire Matthews | 09/1999 | 07/2001 | Religious Studies |
| Mr Edward Mwanza | 09/1999 | 08/2004 | Chemistry |
| Mrs Mercy Mwanza | 09/1999 | 08/2004 | Hostel parent |
| Mr Gilliard Ngulube | 01/2000 | 12/2006 | Building Supervisor |
| Mrs Hilda Ngulube | 01/2000 | 12/2006 | Lab Technician, reprographics |
| Mr Andy Ward | 01/2000 | 09/2000 | Design and Technology |
| Mr Stephen Bannister | 09/2000 | | Sports Master |
| Mrs Chenelle MacMaster | 09/2000 | | Primary teacher |
| Mr Colin MacMaster | 09/2000 | | Outdoor Education |
| Miss Brenda Mumba | 09/2000 | 06/2001 | Caterer |
| Miss Peggy Mwanza | 09/2000 | 03/2003 | History |
| Mr Thomas Kumwenda | 01/2001 | | Maths, 6th Form Hostel parent |
| Miss Pauline Mackendrick | 01/2001 | 08/2005 | Economics, Business Studies |
| Mrs Mary Mwiche | 02/2001 | 12/2003 | Religious Studies |
| Mr Ngosa Mwiche | 02/2001 | 12/2004 | Accountant |
| Mr Joseph Lubwika | 05/2001 | 08/2006 | French |
| Mrs Priscilla Mwanza | 05/2001 | | Geography |
| Mr Willedy Mwanza | 05/2001 | | Technical Subjects |
| Mrs Mollie Roff | 05/2001 | | Textiles |
| Mr Trevor Roff | 05/2001 | | English |
| Miss Julia Symons | 05/2001 | 04/2004 | Outdoor Education Manager |
| Mr Chris Chichoni | 08/2001 | 11/2003 | Buyer |
| Mrs Vasty Chichoni | 08/2001 | 11/2003 | Accounts Assistant |
| Mrs Annie Lubwika | 09/2001 | | Hostel parent |
| Mrs Sanana Mbaleni | 09/2001 | 12/2004 | Primary Teacher |
| Mrs Coral Young | 09/2001 | | Heads' secretary |
| Mr Peter Matthews | 01/2002 | | Physics |
| Mr Benson Mukabe | 01/2002 | 03/2003 | Workshop supervisor —deceased |
| Mrs Edna Muwowo | 01/2002 | | Pre-school teacher, hostel parent |
| Mr Trywell Muwowo | 01/2002 | | Hostel parent |
| Miss Agatha Phiri | 01/2002 | 12/2005 | P.E. |
| Dr Kit Bunker | 04/2002 | 03/2004 | Physics |
| Miss Delwyn Houghton | 04/2002 | | Music, Hostel parent |
| Mr Alex Britton | 09/2002 | 12/2004 | Outdoor Education |
| Mr Weston Chibuye | 09/2002 | | Primary teacher |
| Mr Andrew Cowling | 09/2002 | | Deputy Head, History |
| Mrs Naomi Cowling | 09/2002 | | Primary, Special Needs |
| Miss Sarah Guyton | 09/2002 | | Horse riding, Community Service |
| Miss Mary Hanson | 09/2002 | 08/2004 | Primary teacher |
| ditto. | 01/2003 | 07/2003 | Sports teacher |
| Mrs Anne Alford | 01/2003 | | French |
| Mr Charles Alford | 01/2003 | | Chemistry, Deputy Head |
| Mrs Jane Manongo | 09/2003 | | Cashier |

| | | | |
|---|---|---|---|
| Lt. Col. Moses Manongo | 09/2003 | | Human Resources Officer |
| Mrs Anita Solomon | 09/2003 | | English |
| Mr Daniel Solomon | 09/2003 | | Caterer |
| Mrs Louisa Dawes | 10/2003 | | History |
| Mr Rob Dawes | 10/2003 | | Biology, Science Agricultural Science |
| Mrs Gardiner Mukuni | 01/2004 | | Religious Studies |
| Mr Warren Mukuni | 01/2004 | | Primary teacher |
| Mrs Jane Ngula | 01/2004 | | Office Assistant |
| Mr Muphana Ngula | 01/2004 | | Accountant |
| Mr Elton Nyirenda | 01/2004 | | Music, hostel parent |
| Mr Francis Sichinga | 01/2004 | | P.E., hostel parent |
| Mr Richard Banda | 02/2004 | | Clinical Officer |
| Mr Nelson Phiri | 04/2004 | 05/2004 | Agriculture |
| Mr Beatus Nshenda | 05/2004 | 08/2004 | Physics |
| Mrs Sarah Banda | 06/2004 | | Domestic Supervisor |
| Mr Chinsensele Nsobaula | 06/2004 | | Accounts |
| Mr George Mainza | 07/2004 | 08/2006 | Buyer |
| Miss Caroline Mubangalala | 07/2004 | | Outdoor Education trainee |
| Mrs Anne Jordan | 09/2004 | | Primary Teacher |
| Mr Stephen Jordan | 09/2004 | | Primary Head |
| Mr Boniface Kalilanji | 09/2004 | | Careers |
| Mr Brian Mather | 09/2004 | 12/2005 | Secondary Head |
| Mr Jani Zabangwa | 11/2004 | | Head Staff Development & External relations |
| Mrs Lynette Zabangwa | 11/2004 | | Geography |
| Mrs Angela Hannay | 01/2005 | | Primary Hostel parent |
| Mr Paul Hannay | 01/2005 | | Maintenance Supervisor |
| Mrs Vester Kalilanji | 01/2005 | | Hostel parent |
| Mr Mollet Vwalika | 01/2005 | | Primary teacher |
| Mr Jerran Phiri | 03/2005 | 08/2006 | Maths |
| Mrs Teni Mainza | 04/2005 | 08/2006 | Admin assistant |
| Mr Nelson Phiri | 06/2005 | | Biology teacher |
| Mrs Njiba Kumwenda | 09/2005 | | Reprographics Assistant |
| Mr Pyela Zimba | 09/2005 | | Buyer |
| Mrs Lorna Renaux | 01/2006 | | Biology teacher |
| Miss Grace Yaonga | 01/2006 | | P.E. teacher |

# Appendix 2

## Map of Chengelo Campus

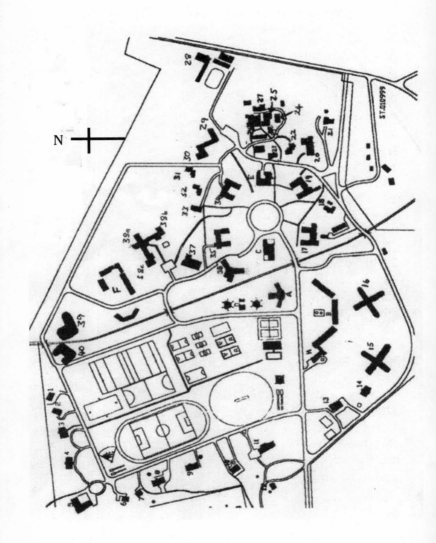

## KEY TO THE MAP OF CHENGELO CAMPUS

A      Administrative Block
B      Classrooms
C      Library
D      Design and Technology Centre
E      Dining Room
F      Primary School
H      Sixth form
1-11,13,14,18,21-27,31-33,39,40 are staff houses
15,16  Sixth form girls and boys hostels resp.
17    Junior Boys Hostel
19    Senior Boys Hostel
20    Form 5 Boys Hostel
28    Stables
29,30  Nurses' houses and Clinic,
34    Junior Girls Hostel
35    Senior Girls Hostel
36    Form 5 Girls Hostel
37    The younger primary hostel with
       houseparents accomodation attached
38    The older primary hostel with
       a,b,c houseparent accomodation units attached

The square box above unit 23 is the stores.
The rectangle to the right of this is the old prefab classrooms which are being re-converted into two staff units of accomodation.

# About the Author

Jeremy Collingwood was educated at Pangbourne Nautical College and Corpus Christi College, Cambridge. After graduating, he worked in Zambia for nine years as a district officer, magistrate, and Head of the Law School at the National Institute of Public Administration in Lusaka.

On returning to England, he was employed as a barrister with the Director of Public Prosecutions in London. He was ordained into the Anglican ministry in 1978, and served as a vicar and rural dean in Bristol and Guildford. He has led a number of teaching missions in South Africa, Uganda, Tanzania and Zambia. He is now in pensioned ministry and retains a close interest in Africa and Zambia in particular. He is married, with three daughters and five grandchildren.

He is the author of *Criminal Law of East and Central Africa*, London: Sweet and Maxwell, 1967; (with his wife Margaret) *Hannah More*, Oxford: Lion, 1990; *Francis Paynter: A Remarkable Guildfordian*, 2001; and various legal, theological and historical articles.

# Index